ALIENS OVER AMERICA

Cover Illustration: Dean Deakyne
Cover Design: Jay Zeballos
Editing: Carlo Panno
Typesetting: Mike Zeballos

Library of Congress Catalog Card Number 99-96425
ISBN 0-9675632-0-8

FIRST EDITION: January 2000

ALIENS OVER AMERICA

Twelve Fantastic Books Reviewed
Including Interviews With Authors

Timothy Guy

AOA
PRESS

california

To Tom, brother, inspiration

Preface

One January, I placed the following ad in a local paper:

U.F.O.s
If you've had a UFO encounter
in the San Fernando Valley
Call 818-xxx-xxxx
for details

The response was tremendous. The San Fernando Valley was apparently a hotbed of UFO activity. I quickly discovered that many citizens are now convinced that the U.S. Government is holding onto a major UFO secret. But we did see panic in the streets when Orson Welles broadcast his fake Martian attack, so what's a Government to do?

If you live and work in the 3-D world, you will want to read this book to see just how close UFOs are to you. And UFOs are every-where. This review of twelve fantastic books—including interviews with authors—presents you with pieces of the puzzle. How you put them together is up to you.

To those of you who are afraid: the more we know about some-thing, the less we fear. Daniel Webster once wrote that education is a teacher sitting on one end of a log and a student on the other. Everything else tends to get in the way.

Today, you're sitting on that log, book in hand.

Twelve teachers await you.

Let's begin their stories.

Table of Contents

Aliens Over America

*W*e had the sky up, up there, all speckled with stars, and we used to lay on our backs and look up at them and discuss about whether they was made or only just happened.

—MARK TWAIN'S *Huckleberry Finn*

Chapter One

The Strange Case of Dr. Stranges

He heard his first UFO story

at age 28 –

He met an alien from Venus

at age 32 –

And now at the age of 70 –

that alien is telling him

the time is getting "ripe"

The End Times are nigh...

The Strange Case
of Dr. Stranges

An unfortunate name for such an unusual man. Or perhaps not. The figure lecturing from the podium is Dr. Frank Stranges [St-rán-ges], a short, stocky man with white hair and a short-cropped silver beard. An ordained minister since 1950, Stranges is a former National Chaplain for the National Association of Police Chiefs, who has found himself in the midst of a trend of conspiracies. "In the U.S. Government today," asserts Stranges, "UFO secrecy is on the rampage."

Case in point: The Air Force's "Project Blue Book" was shut down and its files closed due to lack of interest.

Lack of interest? With *E.T.* and *Independence Day* and *Star Wars* being three of the biggest films of all times? With the numerous TV shows and album covers and books portraying extraterrestrials? With claims of sightings, landings and personal encounters being reported daily?

Why all the Government secrecy? That's what Stranges wants to know, and for the past thirty-five years, he's been looking to find out why. As founder and president of NICUFO (National Investigations Committee on UFOs), Stranges is now recognized as an important contributor to the understanding of the UFO phenomenon.

Dr. Frank Stranges (Courtesy of Frank Stranges)

Stranges is also proud that Ronald Reagan holds membership card #1 in his NICUFO organization. As he points out in his lectures, why did President Reagan refer to an alien presence in his speeches, not once, but five times? Reagan even stood before a United Nations Assembly to explain the Strategic Defense Initiative (also known as "Star Wars") as designed not to protect the U.S. from the Russians, but to defend the whole planet against alien invasion.

Stranges claims that every President from Truman to Bush, and he met with most of them, have all had UFO experiences, but from the moment that they take the oath of office, the Intelligence Agencies inform them that they do not have the liberty to do and say what they want. There is a power *behind* the White House, one that stays even when the administration changes.

Stranges reminds us that in his farewell speech, President Nixon said that he was going to tell the American people the truth about UFOs, and then didn't. And Jimmy Carter had his own UFO encounter while Governor of Georgia, filing a seven-page report about a glowing object that hovered the Georgia skies for twelve minutes. During his election campaign, Carter pledged to open all UFO files if elected. Carter was elected, and soon after, newspapers were hinting that he was preparing to make some "unsettling announcements" about UFOs, but it never happened. To this day, Carter will not say why.

Or take, for example, Senator Barry Goldwater, who in the 1960s asked his friend Gen. Curtis LeMay for access to "Hangar 18" on Wright-Patterson AFB (Dayton, Ohio), where he had heard that UFO wreckage and bodies were being stored. As Chairman of the Senate Intelligence Committee, Goldwater presumably had the clearance to see anything in the military's arsenal. Instead, he said that Gen. LeMay gave him hell for asking, and the Senator's request was denied.

And what's this we hear about Gen. MacArthur telling the *New York Times* back in 1955: "The nations of the world will be forced to unite...for the next war will be an interplanetary war."

"If suddenly there was a threat to this world, from some other species from another planet outside in the Universe, we'd forget all the little local differences that we have between our two countries, and we would find out once and for all that we are all human beings on this Earth."

Ronald Reagan to Mikhail Gorbachev

So why does the U.S. Government not want to reveal what it knows about UFOs? Stranges believes that the fear factor plays a large part: "UFOs violate every known law of aerodynamics. It would be admitting that the U.S. military has no way of defending against them. And the implications concerning virtually all of humanity would be enormous. People might panic. Society could be thrown into chaos."

Stranges points out that the Rand Corporation, a private think tank, was assigned to feed UFO data into a computer, and then enter into an imaginary war with these aliens. Since we did not know where they were coming from, what their technology was, or how to attack their bases, the computer advised planet Earth to surrender.

According to Stranges, the Government's attitude about the alien issue is "We will tell the people only what they should know." This, in a country where the governing is supposed to be of the people, by the people, and for the people! Yet let a good citizen question the authorities about UFOs, and the answer always comes back: "And what is your need to know, sir?"

From the podium Stranges speaks with a sense of urgency. He believes that we the people have to right to the truth, the whole truth and nothing but the truth about UFOs, and that it is the truth that will ultimately set us free—from ignorance, from fear, from superstition. Attend a Stranges lecture, and they are given worldwide, and you will hear his overriding theme: We are on the threshold of a most important event.

How does he know this?

(Courtesy of Universe Publishing)

Stranges has a strange tale to tell. He says that a day in 1959 changed his life forever, when he met Commander Valiant Thor from the planet Venus. In his book *Stranger At The Pentagon*, Stranges writes the Commander's spaceship first landed outside Alexandria, Virginia, in March of 1957, and that Val was taken to the Pentagon where he met with President Eisenhower and Vice-President Nixon. Val told Eisenhower that the world was in a precarious situation and headed for self-destruction.

Eisenhower arranged for Val to appear before the United Nations in a closed session (no documentation available), but the delegates that heard him speak that day were both frightened and angered at what they heard. Val's warnings were considered to be a threat to the political and economic structure of the world, and they declined to take him up on his offer of advice for the human race.

Stranges was lecturing as a Christian minister at the

National Evangelic Center in Washington, D.C., when he was approached by a woman who informed him that Washington had someone they wanted him to meet. In the late '50s, the mystery of UFOs was just beginning to unfold, and Stranges already had a reputation for an interest in the phenomenon.

Stranges says that he was hesitant to go at first, but when she flashed her Pentagon ID, she had his attention. She took him to an underground level beneath the Pentagon, where he was led into an office and introduced to the alien that he would come to know as Commander Valiant Thor— Supreme Commander of the Council Of Twelve. He describes Val as "looking very human, handsome even, standing about six-foot-tall, one hundred and fifty-five pounds, with brown hair and brown eyes. But when we shook hands, he looked right through me."

Commander Valiant Thor– Supreme Commander of the Council of Twelve (Courtesy of Frank Stranges)

Stranges recalls asking the alien the religion of the Space People. Val replied that there is One God of the Universe, the Creator of the Heavens and the Earth, and that they too pray, only with their palms up, looking up into the sky. Stranges asked if they used a Bible, and Val replied, "Why would we need a book when we still walk hand in hand with the Creator?"

Val's proof of his extraterrestrial status? He had no fingerprints! This brings to mind the claim of Genesis 4:15 where Cain killed Abel, and God put a mark on Cain before casting him out of the Garden, so that everyone would know who he was, by his fingerprints. And, in a sense, all of the human race has fingerprints because we are all guilty.

After their meeting, Val returned to his planet, Venus, and Stranges was interrogated by the FBI for three hours about his conversation with the alien. They found Stranges to be as much in the dark as they were as to who Val was and what was his mission.

One year later, Stranges was driving through Beverly Hills, California, when Commander Val suddenly appeared in the back seat of his car. He told Stranges that he had been instructed to return to Earth and monitor the situation, but that he could not interfere or divulge the essence of his mission until "The time is ripe."

Val and Stranges continued their clandestine relationship, and over the ensuing years, Val gave Stranges many insights that led him to investigate mysteries such as the Hollow Earth Theory, the Black Hole, and the Bermuda Triangle. Val revealed to him that Time as we know it is a Place, as in "There is no place like the present."

Val had also written a 64-page manuscript, *Outwitting Tomorrow*, based around the prophecy built into the Great Pyramid, which he considered to be a book, and not a tomb. Val explained to Stranges that he first delivered this book to an American couple twenty years earlier. They took the book and copyrighted it, but then decided that they were too frightened to go public with it. (The story is a fable about a man who must learn to make play out of work, thereby becoming master of his future rather than merely being a puppet of fate.)

In June of 1968, Val had Stranges drive him to a small town in Sonora, Mexico, where they boarded a small boat and went out onto the lake. It was there that Stranges saw his first flying saucer, a 300-foot-diameter disc, 100 feet high at the axis, sitting calmly upon the waters.

"My first impression," Stranges writes, "was one of great exhilaration mingled with joy and excitement. I remembered how my colleagues in the Christian ministry looked with disdain upon such matters as flying saucers and space people, but when it happens to you—I found myself caring less what anyone would think. I was there!"

He was taken aboard the craft and told to disrobe, then placed inside a chamber where he showered without water. He describes it as a purifying sensation all over his body. He was given a white one-piece jumpsuit to wear and he sat down with Val before a large screen, where they watched the presidential campaign celebration for Robert F. Kennedy.

Val told Stranges that he had previously met with Robert Kennedy (rumored to have been a card-carrying member of the "Amalgamated Flying Saucer Clubs of America"). His first impression of Kennedy was that he was a very nervous and suspicious man, and a man who should not be crossed politically. Kennedy queried Val as to his chances for the Presidency, and Val replied, "Mr. Kennedy, four years from now, you will stand an excellent chance of winning. But I beg you to remain far away from the political race this year."

Kennedy apparently ignored the advice, and as Stranges and Val sat watching the presidential campaign taking place at the Ambassador Hotel in Los Angeles, RFK was shot before their very eyes. This is all the more remarkable when you consider the event was not televised.

Stranges claims that Val is still present on Earth, and in command of a fleet of Venusian spaceships assigned to this planet. Val's message to Stranges: Earth is getting ready for a change.

Stranges is still in touch with the Commander ("I talked to him on the phone yesterday"), whose spaceship is parked near the shores of Lake Mead, Nevada (northwest of Hoover Dam, southeast of Nellis Air Force Base, about one mile from the junction of Highways 147 and 166).

Nellis Air Force Base, incidentally, is part of the vast complex known as Dreamland." Although most of the base is reportedly underground, the expanse above ground is known as "Area 51," where America's most advanced aircraft are test-flown.

Stranges says several thousand people know that the spacecraft is there, including two thousand Government officials currently in office. However, don't go running out there looking for it; the spaceship is covered by a force field, rendering it invisible. Even the Air Force, with their radar grids, can't find it.

Verifiable proof is hard to come by in a world of secrets, but Stranges did have one close friend who gave him a glimpse of how vast the secrecy is that's going on around us. Stranges concluded his lecture by turning off the auditorium lights and switching on the projector. This proof was in the form of a photographic slide of his friend standing upon the moon.

That close friend was Astronaut Col. James Irwin, now deceased, who flew the Apollo 15 mission to the moon in 1971. Irwin was the first man to drive a vehicle across the moon's surface. He told Stranges that what he saw on the moon would "stir people to wonder"—domed cities and machinery moving around underground that rippled the moon's surface—but that such things were never reported to the American public.

Col. James Irwin, Apollo 15. Note glow around Irwin standing on the lunar surface, a refraction of light and an indication of atmosphere on the moon? (Courtesy of NASA)

Col. Irwin's proof that things on the moon are not as people were told lay in that photographic slide that he had of himself. As he stands upon the moon, wearing his space suit and helmet, breathing his bottled oxygen, his entire body is surrounded by a halo of light from the camera lights. Not to say that the Colonel was claiming to be saintly, but a halo of diffused light means atmosphere—light reflecting off particles of moisture—yet we've been taught that the moon has no atmosphere!

This is just one of the many atmospheric secrets that Stranges says the U.S. Government is keeping about the nature of the Universe. "But such secrets," concludes Stranges, "are getting harder to keep. We now have atomic microscopes that are beginning to show the average man entire universes previously unseen to the naked eye. Our Universe is only one of many universes that stretch endlessly."

I was able to interview Stranges at his NICUFO Headquarters, located in Van Nuys, California. He's a quiet and reserved man. He is also surrounded by a coterie of people, a wall, so to speak, to protect him from those who would wish to interview him and then poke barbs at him. Luckily, at the lecture, I was able to make a quick friendship with his secretary, who opened some doors for me, and I was offered an interview with Stranges himself. I couldn't pass that up.

Author and Dr. Stranges

Waiting in Stranges' office was like browsing through a museum. Certificates of ancient orders were framed upon the wall, large medals from secret organizations were encased in glass, and a bookshelf lining one wall contained a library of rare UFO and paranormal books. Then Stranges came in to greet me with a handshake, looking distinguished in his three-piece suit. After having watched him lecture—the man is a presence at the podium—I was surprised by his humble demeanor as we sat down for our one-on-one.

He was also skilled at being interviewed. I started off by stating that I didn't wish to ask the same old obvious questions, like "Who is Val?" and "When will you be seeing him again?" He said, "Good." I told him that what I really needed was a couple of killer sidebars, stunner facts about UFOs in America to put in boxes at the side of the page.

"Then why don't you ask me the question this way," Stranges replied. "Ask me: What happened at Edwards Air Force Base [California] when three small silver discs landed on the runway and a small alien got out of one of them, got into one of the other spacecrafts, then they both flew off, leaving the third spacecraft behind?"

Well, since you put it that way, what *did* happen at Edwards AFB on that fateful day?

"President Eisenhower was immediately flown out to Palm Springs with his wife under the auspices of taking a vacation, and he was then helicoptered out to the Edwards base and shown the spacecraft. As he was standing there, the craft glowed, then dematerialized, then seconds later it reappeared, and Eisenhower had a heart attack."

As the story goes, Eisenhower later signed some kind of treaty with these aliens, allowing them to use some of our military bases in exchange for them sharing their technology with us. The U.S. apparently had no choice but to sign the agreement as the ETs' technology was far superior to ours. Thus it's theorized that Eisenhower formed Majestic 12 (MJ-12) as a clandestine group designed to deal with the alien presence. Many UFO researchers believe that Eisenhower was the last president to know the entire alien situation.

Stranges himself had recently made the news when the Heaven's Gate mass suicide took place. Thirty-eight disciples had followed their leader in abandoning their "vehicles" in order to rendezvous with a spaceship supposedly following in the wake of the Comet Hale-Bopp. Stranges began receiving phone calls from newspapers and magazines around the world, including *Time* and *Newsweek*. Apparently, he's considered the Californian authority on UFOs and cult nuts. I asked him what the story was behind these burgeoning New Age cults.

"One must go back to the beginning of organized religion, when the populace was first taught to worship God out of fear, not out of

love. Cult members fear their leaders, not
love them, and so they are easily misled."
What happens when a cult grows too large to be called a
cult? Do they self-destruct, or become a religion?
"I believe that most religions today are self-
destructing."
In your book, you write, "The Universe is alive with evidence of God's footsteps in the skies. Meanwhile on Earth,
churches are losing ground as young people are becoming dis-
illusioned with their religious organizations. Morals are lax,
society is whirling in chaos, and that an event of some magni-
tude will be needed to bring about a change." You add,
however, that Commander Val has predicted an eventual happy
outcome for Mankind.
"That's why Commander Val is here, to assist
in this eventual positive outcome."
Is Val an angel?
"Commander Val is not an angel. One example is that Val is married, and angels don't
marry."
When will Commander Val begin his agenda in regard to
this spiritual advancement of humankind?
"No one knows the time. Even Val takes
orders from a Higher Source."
But when that time does come...?
"When the time is ripe, his first worldwide
appearance will be at the United Nations,
this time in an open and televised session."
And what will he say?
"He'll dispense his advice."
You also warn in your books that all UFOs are not friendly.
"There are good aliens, and there are evil
aliens, which is one of the reasons why the
Government won't admit to UFOs. They'll
tell you that there are no such things as
UFOs, only people who claim to have seen
one. But the correct translation of John 14:2

in the New Testament is 'In my Father's
house, there are many Universes.' The hand
of God extends far beyond that which our
feeble minds can comprehend."

Here then is my question: You're out there trying to spread
the word about UFOs and the End Times, but if Val says that the
time is not ripe, and refuses to do anything until the time is
right, what good is your continued marching on?

"I still have my duties as a Minister to assist
in spreading the Word of God. But also I'm
hoping to be a part of the worldwide awakening to the Golden Rule."

And why did Commander Val choose you to contact?

"I have no answer for that other than 'Seek
and ye shall find,' and I have always been a
seeker."

Does Val have any advice for the human race?

"Pray. Other than that, the history of Man is
in its Final Chapter."

Do you think that you'll be around to see these End Times?

"Yes, absolutely. I believe it will be before I
pass away." [Stranges was born in 1927.]

After the interview, Stranges and I had our picture taken
together. But as I drove myself home, I got to thinking about
this whole UFO cover-up conspiracy. It's an intrigue of enormous proportions. What if the Government does possess ET
technology? Why are they hiding it? And how is this secrecy so
easy to keep? All we ever seem to hear are leaks.

And it does strike this writer that no one else in the entire
NICUFO organization except Stranges has met this Commander
Val Thor, meaning, of course, that Stranges himself must be part
of the conspiracy. However, Stranges does have much to offer.
That slide that he showed us of Col. Irwin standing there in
atmosphere on the moon is certainly a puzzler. And that
account of Val having no fingerprints is rather unique, a more
than satisfying explanation as to what that mark was that God

put on killer Cain before casting him out of the Garden of Eden.

But then I asked myself:

(1) On what date did President Eisenhower first meet with Commander Val at the White House? My point being that if Eisenhower had already met Val, there would be no reason to have a heart attack upon seeing the flying saucers at Edwards AFB. Or if Eisenhower had seen the spaceships first, why would he not then listen to the advice of Val the alien?

(2) Help me here: On what date was Robert Kennedy a card-carrying member of Amalgamated Flying Saucers? My point being that if Commander Val warned RFK not to run for the Presidency, why would Kennedy not listen to a spaceman? Even a Kennedy would have to listen to an alien with no fingerprints.

So I called Stranges' office the next day to ask him, but he was not in and did not return my call. I don't blame him. He can only tell the story as he's heard it.

The secrecy goes on.

Chapter Two

The Real
Space Cadet

In his past life –

    he was an outlaw

    who was tortured in prison

Jack London wrote a book about him

And now –

    that outlaw is back

    and writing his own books

    on the paranormal

The Real
Space Cadet

The name of the first book in this cosmic saga is *The Star Rover* by Jack London. Ask any student of literature today if they've read or even heard of this book by one of America's greatest writers, and they will most likely tell you no.

It is perhaps his greatest work.

Briefly put, *The Star Rover* was a fictionalized account of the true story of Ed Morrell (born 1896), a small-time criminal who was sentenced to life imprisonment for an assorted number of crimes. Once inside prison walls, Morrell was implicated in a gun-smuggling scheme to advance a prison break. He denied knowing where the guns were and so "solitary confinement for the rest of your life" was his sentence, or at least until he revealed where the guns were.

Morrell was taken down into a dungeon and thrown into a small cell with a stone floor. It was there that the warden, known as "The Pirate" for the patch that he wore over one eye, introduced him to one of the most hideous torture devices ever known to man—the straitjacket.

They placed Morrell's arms inside the long sleeves, then wrapped him up in its constricting folds. The guard then braced his foot against Morrell's back, pulled the rope tighter and fastened it with a knot. The canvas device is designed to squeeze the life out of its victim, inch by inch, in unbearable pain. When Morrell screamed in agony, he was gagged then left to lie alone upon the floor. There in the darkness and the dampness of his cell, hidden away from the rest of the world, he began to experience the excruciating torture of the jacket.

THE STAR ROVER
BY JACK LONDON

The Great Reincarnation Novel
New Epilogue By Dick Sutphen: The True Story Behind The Book

(Courtesy of Valley of the Sun Publishing)

This kind of cruelty was no anomaly in America's brutal penal system. As Morrell wrote in his own book, *The 25th Man*, "All countries have their history of fiendish tortures designed to make its victims cry aloud to Heaven for mercy." Our prisons at that time were "dark and loathsome cells...leg irons and chains...brutal guards and whipping posts." It was the rod iron for all lawbreakers. Prisons were places where after the "interrogation," the prisoner usually had to be dragged back to his cell, babbling and delirious, if not unconscious.

Morrell relates that he had not been in the jacket fifteen minutes when sharp needle-like sensations began shooting through his feet and hands from the tightening pressure of the jacket. A feeling of horror overwhelmed him as the prickling sensation spread into his arms and legs. "I was seized by a sense of suffocation similar to the experience of being buried alive. It was not as Jack London would write it up—inch by inch, joint by joint, and then the rest of the body, but my entire body went numb at once."

Morrell was left to lie there in the straitjacket for four and a half days (with bread and water once a day, just enough to keep him alive). He was unable to sleep for the entire duration as the pain of his body being slowly crushed to a pulp kept him awake. And he could feel burning pain where his urine and excrement were eating away into his skin like acid.

By the time the warden returned to the cell and ordered the straitjacket removed, Morrell's entire body was bleeding, and he found that he could not move. After this first torture session was over, Morrell was left lying paralyzed and utterly helpless on the stone floor of his cell. "I was nothing but a mass of bruised flesh and bone."

"Until now," Morrell writes, "I had always felt that there

Ed Morrell (Courtesy of New Era Publishing)

was a way out, but the straitjacket had brought me to complete despair. I did not then know that some people are called upon to pay a terrific penalty in order to bring out a true understanding of their inherent goodness.

"I slept...mine was a strange sleep..." and as Morrell lay there in his delirium, he heard "a voice, far far away at first, until it finally seemed to speak plain in my ear saying—'You have learned the futility of trying to fight off your enemies with hatred. From today, a new life vista will open up and you will fight from a far superior vantage point, and this new weapon will cut and hew away all evil forces which now oppose you. And to prove this power to you, even the straitjacket will have no terrors for you. It will only be a means to greater things.'"

When the Pirate returned, Morrell still could not tell him where the guns were, so again he was placed in the straitjacket. This time, however, Morrell's experience was much different.

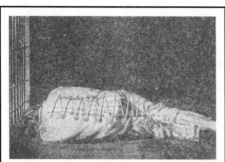

Ed Morrell, Jack London's "Star Rover" in the San Quentin straightjacket (Courtesy of New Era Publishing)

As he lay bound and motionless upon the cold floor in his dark cell, terrified inside the tightly-laced jacket, his body being squeezed numb, Morrell had an out-of-body experience. Today we call it "astral projection," but in the early 1900s, it was a mystery to Morrell as to how his spirit was able to slip out of his tortured body and leave its pain behind.

Morrell writes: "Now I was out of my jacket, bending down looking at my body. A great pity welled up within me. There on the floor lay a wreck of a man. His hair was matted and he had a shaggy beard. I could see his two eyes shining like black coals. I felt the urge to watch and safeguard it with the vigilance of a sentry."

Out-of-body, Morrell found that he could travel anywhere in the world, even going back in time to relive past lives. He saw that people on the city streets each possessed a different odor. He saw that some people wore a happy smile and had a bright light diffusing around their heads, while others had a foul odor and faces almost obscured by dark shadows. As his soul wandered through "a living, breathing world" outside of his physical body, he lost all consciousness of time and space. It enabled him to survive his insanity while undergoing the torture.

"I was indeed the 'star rover' of Jack London's book," Morrell writes. "He called those experiences 'the living death.' I prefer to call them 'my new life in tune with a power divine.' Before being placed into the jacket, I was seething with hatred for every one of them, cursing them, vowing vengeance. Strange to say now I looked at them with deep compassion instead of hatred."

When the warden and his guards returned, they found

Morrell was actually refreshed. And since he could tell them nothing of the hidden guns, Morrell was time and again subjected to the ghastly torture of the jacket, the rope fitting tighter and tighter around his shriveled body. Each time, Morrell's mind was able to slip away from the pain as his soul eased out into a disassociated state, leaving his body behind "snug as a bug in a rug."

"The dungeon no longer represented to me a place of damnation and torment," writes Morrell. "Wonderful to relate, I had found that my mind and body were entirely separate." On one occasion, Morrell "weathered the storm" for one hundred and twenty-six continuous hours of constriction in the straitjacket, the longest torture ever inflicted on an innate in San Quentin.

Morrell's astral projections took him to places where he saw events that he was later able to corroborate. He also found himself repeatedly drawn to a young schoolgirl sitting in a classroom with her schoolmates: "I walked slowly down the aisle and stopped near her desk. She raised her head as if to look at me. She was a little Miss of twelve or thirteen." He ended up following her home, where "she stood at the gate for a moment, pensive, then turned and skipped across the yard and entered the house." It was his first of many visits to her that he said helped to ease the burden of his misery in San Quentin.

It was also during these astral projections that he visited the "jails of the nation...cesspools of iniquity...horrible...inconceivable...all of them bad. I saw hundreds of thousands of human beings in idleness...being educated in unique ways of crime...taught nothing constructive...drifting in and out of prison at taxpayers' expense.

"The revelation came to me right there, the vision which I was to build the system which I have chosen to call 'The New Era Penology.' My vision was that some men, especially if they're illiterate like I myself was, would never get anywhere if left to themselves. Prisons must provide learning and vocational training."

Morrell suffered through his solitary confinement and torture, without human companionship, for a full five years. Then a change of wardens led to an investigation of his situation, and he was suddenly removed from solitary. His straitjacket years and his astral projections were behind him. Four years later, after fifteen years in prison, Morrell was handed a pardon.

He looked at himself in a mirror for the first time in years, his body weighing in at only ninety-six pounds in all its shriveled horribleness. He was a wreck of a human being, and he wondered if he would ever have his health again. And, of course, everyone wanted to get a look at the "Dungeon Man."

He writes: "And then I cried. And I vowed henceforth I would rely with the simple faith of a child in God's protection that surrounded me, and which had been made manifest when my jackets were stretched asunder and I was saved from death."

Upon his release from prison, Morrell began campaigning for prison reform, giving lectures around the country, hoping to awaken the public's conscience to the truly brutal prison system going on behind their prison walls.

Jack London (circa 1910)

That's when Jack London heard about the story, and he decided to work Morrell's experiences into a novel. London hired a young journalism student to attend Morrell's lectures and sit and take notes. Morrell quickly recognized her as the young girl in the classroom that he had so often astral projected to years earlier while in the straitjacket. The girl also recognized Morrell as the distraught man who had appeared to her in her apparitions. She was an adult now, and she eventually became Mrs. Ed Morrell.

When London's resulting novel *The Star Rover* was published, it was immediately panned. In 1915, any book about astral projection and reincarnation was bound to be thrashed by the critics, and it was. It went quickly out of print.

But it did inspire Morrell to tell his own story. He and his young wife started a publishing company, and Morrell wrote his own story in a book called *The 25th Man.* (Morrell had been the twenty-fifth man to join a gang of railroad thieves that eventually got him arrested.)

Actually, his wife wrote the book, as Morrell was illiterate. They also founded "The American Crusaders For The Advancement of The New Era Penology," based on the concept that he first thought up while in the straitjacket. The organization worked on initiating major prison reform, making them corrective systems and not destructive ones.

When *The 25th Man* appeared in print, the public became outraged at its revelations, and the country as a whole began taking a closer look at its penal institutions. Morrell was called before the U.S. Congress, stunning his listeners with his tales of horror, prompting many states to begin enacting laws that would stop the inhumane brutality going on behind their prison walls.

All this can be said to be the direct result of London's groundbreaking novel *The Star Rover.* Few have heard of it, fewer have read it, but any time a book can expose an injustice, and help to rectify that injustice, it stands as a classic testament to the power of the written word.

It's an incredible story. And it doesn't stop there.

In 1965, Dick Sutphen wrote his first book, then started his own publishing company to investigate and write about reincarnation and metaphysics. The purpose of his company was to promote books on self-improvement and the coming New Age. His publishing company was certainly many years ahead of its time.

*Dick Sutphen (Courtesy of
Valley of the Sun Publishing)*

In 1975, a psychic told Sutphen that he had been sent to prison in a past life, "But because of this, you met Jack London, and it had a strong influence on you being a writer." Sutphen interpreted this to mean that he met London in jail, and since London had been jailed twice (once for poaching, once for vagrancy), he checked the jail accounts but found no clues.

Then one day, synchronicity led a friend to recommend that Sutphen read a novel about reincarnation called *The Star Rover*, if he could find the out-of-print book. He found the book, and read it, and it caused him to search out Ed Morrell's *The 25th Man*. Upon reading it, Sutphen immediately recognized himself as Morrell. Sutphen bought the rights to *The Star Rover* and republished it as a way of saying thank you to London.

One noteworthy fact: Morrell died at the age of 78 in North Hollywood, California, in 1947. Sutphen was already ten years old by then. How can that be?

(Sutphen's most likely explanation might be that time is not linear—all things happen simultaneously—and all past lives are being lived "parallel" to one another and happening at the same time.)

I was able to interview Sutphen in his office at his Valley Of The Sun Publishing company in Malibu, California. At sixty years of age, he stands a lean and handsome six foot one. His office was modern and comfortable, with an open view through his second-story picture window. Most of his CD collection was country music.

I started off by explaining that when I first contacted his office, I had no idea what to expect, half-expecting to see him bedridden, still recuperating from that last incarnation. He laughed and said that he granted

Author and Dick Sutphen

this interview because when he read my inquiry letter with my first question, he knew that I was serious.

Then let's start with that first question: If in the darkness of his dungeon, Morrell discovered his "True Self," why would he—who suffered terribly to presumably pay for his sins, and who experienced such enlightenment that he went out and achieved something positive in the world—why would a man like this need another incarnation on this planet? I find this disheartening.

"Ed Morrell, as do all of us," Sutphen replied, "had a lot of things to balance in a short time. That's awfully hard to do, because who can achieve perfection in one lifetime?"

So Morrell's suffering helped propel him along the spiritual path of life?

"I believe so. We discover spiritual values by passing through spiritual ordeals. This is how we shape our own destiny."

Jack London wrote in his *The Star Rover*: "There is no death. Life is spirit and spirit cannot die." If this is true, can we ever hope to break our karmic fate?

"If you really want to know your karma, look at your fears, your fear-based emotions. Ed Morrell may have resolved a lot of karma, but

it doesn't mean he necessarily resolved all of
his fear-based emotions. He still fears."

Can you give an example?

"Any negative emotion inside of you is based
on a fear, be it your anger or pessimism or
even your boredom. Boredom, for example,
is a loud message. It's saying: I'm living
wrong!"

Sutphen's enthusiasm about his message is backed up by
the fact that since 1976, over 125,000 people have attended his
seminars and workshops. His workshops are short on talk, with
emphasis on class participation in exploring altered states.
They are about self-improvement and developing the psychic
mind. Does he consider himself to be naturally psychic?

"No, I do not feel I'm naturally psychic,
although to some degree, we all are. But I do
know that through practice and proper tech-
nique, it's definitely something we can all
learn. In fact, in the countless regressions
I've done [through hypnosis] in taking people back to Atlantis—telepathy was a way of
life then—these subjects say that it is precisely because of this lack of telepathy in our
society today that we feel so lonely."

You're saying that in today's society, people feel alienated
from one another because of our psychic inability.

"Exactly. And one of the goals of my seminars is to guide the individual to become
aware of their self-defeating attitudes, the
saying of 'I can't.' We each build our own
walls. Everything that we think, say, and do
creates karma. And our karma is really our
fears."

I mentioned that while I was sitting in his lobby, I picked
up one of his catalogues, and I could see that he runs a small
publishing empire. He laughed.

"I started my career playing around with

hypnosis tapes, making my own tapes and experimenting with them. Then I started sending them [pre-recorded hypnosis tapes] to nearby Florence Penitentiary to teach the prisoners there how to astral project. For some reason, I empathized with them. Talk about your synchronicity. It wasn't until years later that I found out about the Ed Morrell story. That was a stunner for me."

And today your company produces audio and video tapes that help develop psychic abilities.

"Subliminal tapes can support your goal, but it still takes practice, practice—like anything else—practice."

Many of your books and seminars deal with man-woman relationships, especially viewed in the light of reincarnation. They seem aimed at people who are not finding the right mate.

"I tell them: Look around you. Your best mirror for learning to respond to life in a harmonious flow are in your relationships with family, friends, in-laws, co-workers."

Pocket Books has labeled you "America's Foremost Psychic Researcher." However, this is a book about UFOs, so I have to ask the question: Any UFO sightings to report?

"No, but I do believe. A close friend of mine is Brad Steiger. He alone has me believing, always keeping me updated with intriguing bits of information and new revelations. But ultimately, what can we do about it? So sit back and watch."

And your beliefs about a Creator?

"Zen would be my closest answer. Zen is accepting responsibility for your emotions. It's accepting 'what is'—what is in fact now—and rising above resistance. Resistance is a waste of strength. Zen, therefore, would be a process and not a religion."

What is the first step in that process to Godhood?
> "Love and understanding. They are the eternal keys to overcoming everything negative. Otherwise, the more you resist, the more it is drawn to you."

And one final question: Any nightmares of that Morrell lifetime?
> "I have dreamed of snatches of that lifetime, but like all nightmares, they're something each of us must deal with, no matter who you are. It's mainly a claustrophobic type of feeling for me."

Undoubtedly, a fear-based emotion, I said.

He laughed, and his secretary came in to snap a picture of the two of us. I followed Sutphen down the staircase into a warehouse where he selected a generous assortment of books and tapes that he thought I might like. I was impressed that this could actually be the Dungeon Man walking around the warehouse, profusely offering me gifts. And the books and tapes that I brought home with me were all positive titles, as if his catalogue is a celebration to the power of positive thinking.

Sutphen left me with the impression that life is real...life is earnest. "Throw a pebble, create a ripple." We pay for our fears. Does this mean that we hold our own keys? If so, with all of our bad karma pouring down, where does our free will come in? The noose seems always still around our necks. My notes seemed inadequate to answer these questions.

Later that night, though, as the day began to resurface, one of the first things that I recalled was Sutphen reciting his favorite Zen quote to me: "You are what you think, having become what you thought." And I thought back on Morrell lying there in the straitjacket in his cell, and thinking spiritual positive happy thoughts. And here was Sutphen today, pleasantly successful, so it must pay off.

But then that very first question of mine came nagging back to me. If Ed Morrell suffered terribly to pay for his sins, discovered his True Self, then went out and did something positive in this world—and he *still* had to reincarnate—what chance do the rest of us have?

I do find this disheartening.

The Star Rover (1915)
(Valley of the Sun Publishing, 1983)
        Jack London

The 25th Man (1924) by Ed Morrell
        is out of print, but enquire at
        your local library.

For a listing of books and tapes, write to:
        Valley of the Sun Publishing
        P.O. Box 38
        Malibu, California 90265

        www.dicksutphen.com

Chapter Three

The Martian Chronicles—Revisited

A remote viewer meditates

into a trance state

Instructions direct his vision

up into the stars

where he is drawn to Mars

And he returns with the word –

there is extraterrestrial life

lots of it

The Martian Chronicles – Revisited

{A beginning note: Subspace should be understood as a dimension other than the physical realm. Your "soul," for example, would exist in subspace; linear time does not. In subspace, all events happen simultaneously, although this makes little sense to those of us standing on Earth, where time follows a sequential path - one minute after another.}

It began for Dr. Courtney Brown in 1992 when he took an advanced course in Transcendental Meditation. He had received a research grant from Emory University to investigate whether meditation could relieve enough stress to reduce conflict in the world.

He began his research by enrolling in the Transcendental Mediation-Sidhi Program, taught by Sidhis who were personally trained by Maharishi Mahesh Yogi himself. Brown describes meditation as a state where intellectual activity diminishes until all of the senses are silent. What remains is not an empty mind but what meditators call a "field of consciousness."

By transcending the five physical senses, one perceives life as nonphysical. It is through this self-realization that the individual can see the Oneness of all life. By the time Brown had completed the course, he was convinced that scientists all over the world should be meditating and studying its beneficial effects.

He then enrolled in the Gateway Voyage Program at the Monroe Institute in Faber, Virginia, to continue his explorations into deeper realms of consciousness. Robert Monroe, founder of the Monroe Institute, is considered a pioneer in exploring out-of-body experiences. He is also known for his work involving the effects of sound waves upon human behavior.

The Gateway course teaches about altered states of consciousness via brain wave techniques. The technology is based upon using sounds to cause frequencies that resonate between the right and left hemispheres of the brain to alter consciousness. The Monroe Institute has apparently found a way of producing actual physical changes in the electrochemical signals that occur in the brain. This extensive course was considered a prerequisite for the U.S. Army's remote viewing training program.

Brown wanted to duplicate the known road of the military's training program, and so he took and successfully completed the Gateway course. Then circumstances led him to a man who had formerly been a member of the Army's remote viewing unit. The military's interest in remote viewing lay in the collecting of information about the country's enemies.

(©1996 Henry Yee, courtesy of Dutton Books)

"Remote viewing," writes Brown in his book *Cosmic Voyage*, "is when information about a target comes to a trained individual through his or her unconscious mind. It involves seeing objects at a considerable distance through the use of one's inner eye, hoping to extract descriptive information about a physical site through the passive act of observation."

The Army's remote viewing program followed a rigorous and exacting set of protocols developed specifically for espionage purposes. The recruits who learned this art served as a highly-classified team of special operations and intelligence officers. Eventually, this program of training "disciplined psychics" came to be known as "Stargate."

Interestingly enough, while the U.S. Military Intelligence picked servicemen and tried to train them to be psychics, the Soviets scoured the countryside for natural psychics and tried to train them for Military Intelligence. Both programs were, apparently, unsuccessful. At least the rate of success was not high enough to warrant further funding on the USA side.

The Army's remote viewing program was supposedly cancelled, and these trained "viewers" were discharged from the service, returning home with the "gift of sight." When a certain ex-military officer opened up a private training program for SRV – Scientific Remote Viewing – Brown was his second student to enroll.

Brown describes the SRV training as an intensive seven-day, six-hours-a-day course. It takes place in a grey room with no bright colors to distract. The purpose of the drab atmosphere is to pacify. Brown writes: "One must remember that the unconscious is highly intelligent but it most definitely must be tamed and trained. Patience is a learned virtue."

The trainer was also a patient person, for it took a while to build up the trust that Brown needed to go further into a trance. Eventually, however, they made progress in taking him into deeper levels of consciousness, states far deeper than hypnosis.

Then one day, Brown entered into his trance state, his monitor gave him the "target coordinates" (the actual destination was always unknown to Brown), and this time, the first thing that Brown saw was a pyramid. It seemed "solid but hollow at the same time," and his consciousness was drawn inside.

Brown describes what he saw as "humanoids," with human faces but no hair. Humanoids have the same basic body plan as humans, with a cylindrical trunk surmounted by a head, with two arms and two legs attached. These humanoids seemed in a state of panic. Brown's consciousness went back outside of the pyramid, where he saw a volcano erupting. "The scene was utter chaos," he writes. "Lots of people had died, and were dying. People were running. Many were scattered. There was a sense of hopelessness. It was terrible!" Brown was witnessing a catastrophe.

When the remote viewing session ended and Brown returned to normal consciousness, his monitor showed him a NASA satellite photo of Mars. Brown had been sent to the Cydonia region of Mars. Cydonia is home to a cluster of structures known as the "pyramids on Mars," some of them with four sides, others five-sided. A couple of miles away from them is a peculiar formation known as the "Face on Mars." These strange unnatural images had been photographed by the 1976 NASA Viking 1 spacecraft.

The Face on Mars has been described as "a stylized human face turned skyward."

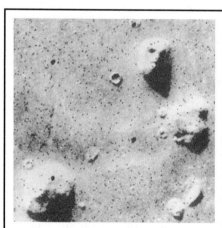

Mars (Cydonia Region)
A trick of light and shadow?
(Courtesy of NASA)

Digital enhancement of the Face shows a "bisymmetrical object having features suggestive of eyes, a nose, and a mouth." Three-dimensional analysis reveals that these facial features remain even when the object is viewed from radically different perspectives.

Fractal Analysis [AT&T Bell Labs, 1993] supports the hypothesis that the Face is artificial and does not belong to the natural terrain. Nor do the numerous pyramids. Wind and water erosion do not cut straight corners. Erosion results in rounded formations.

Brown believes that he had been shown an actual fragment of Martian history. Subsequent remote viewing sessions showed him how this planetary disaster on Mars was caused by a comet passing through its outer atmosphere, not striking the planet, but causing high turbulence. The object caused a circular ripple to form in the atmosphere," Brown writes, "much like a stone dropping into a pool of water forms an expanding circular wave outward. This ripple grew into an atmospheric tidal wave."

After witnessing these "Martian sessions," Brown settled down into his seat, slipped into his altered state, and his monitor gave him a new set of "target coordinates." The monitor listened as Brown described what he saw, and it did not match the description of the preset destination. Instead, it seemed that Brown had been drawn into a deep cavern, where he saw the Martian humanoids now living in a large underground society. He described it as "a virtual city but not a healthy environment, nor was it a happy one. They seemed desperate with their situation. Their children had no future. They seemed to be there only out of a sense of duty."

When Brown returned to normal consciousness, neither he nor his monitor were sure where he had been. After much studying of maps, however, they eventually determined that Brown somehow, for some reason, had been "guided" to Baldy Peak, a mountain located inside a national forest not far from Santa Fe, New Mexico.

"Target coordinates" were redrawn, and subsequent remote viewing sessions took Brown back into the caverns beneath Baldy Peak. He claims that this underground complex is presently serving as a center for numerous other underground Martian bases scattered around the globe, including a major base in Latin America. The planet Mars had suffered a major catastrophe, and although many of the inhabitants died, Brown's remote viewing sessions showed that many were rescued by a group of aliens who came to their aid at the last moment. We know them today as the Greys.

These Greys already had the technology even back then to traverse both Time and Space with great ease. Their rescue was done with great speed, and in the nick of time, and they settled the Martian survivors on the nearest available planet: Earth. Brown claims that these rescuers were the ones who built the

Sphinx in Egypt, whose face gazes back up at the Face on Mars.

Basically, the long and the short of it is, these Martian humanoids are now stuck here on planet Earth. They long ago found Earth's atmosphere inhospitable, so they had to move underground. Today they live in enormous mountainous caverns, hidden away from human hostility, frightened of human aggressiveness. But each generation carries on for the sake of their children and their children's children. They do hold hope for the future.

(Incidentally, Baldy Peak is less than two hundred miles away from Alamogordo, the site of the first atomic bomb test, an explosion which was sure to have awaken the Martians in their cavernous city with the force of, well, an atomic blast.)

Brown writes: "These survivors have needs. Desperate needs. But as it turns out, so do we humans. We will soon need saving ourselves. Bad times are coming for the planet Earth, thanks in large part to Mankind. There will be a period of great struggles. I was shown that there will be a movement off the planet in the future for humans."

Brown believes that many species of aliens will be involved in this evacuation. Collectively, they are known as "The Galactic Federation." The Federation is a subspace organization, meaning they don't live in the physical realm, and most of its members are from the Pleiades star system (the reputed genetic home of Mankind). Although the Federation is much more powerful than us, they need us in a galactic sense.

"At present, however," writes Brown, "Earth humans are considered violent and troublesome and currently unable to cope with the new realities that are approaching. Humans do not see themselves as caretakers of life on this planet, but rather as owners of a garden which is theirs to use. They need to undergo some sort of change before extending far off this planet."

Earth's coming planetary disasters—political, ecological, and nuclear—may help force the human race to transform their attitudes and behaviors, but they must also come to see their new responsibilities as galactic citizens.

And in that sense, it appears that the human species is being prepared for full galactic membership. Entertainments such as *Star Trek* and *Star Wars* have helped human culture to become more open to the complexities of galactic life, especially when they are being watched by so many young people. The Federation wants to help humans to gradually stop thinking that we are alone at the center of the Universe.

In any event, it won't be long before the catastrophes on Earth accelerate. As the ecosystem of the planet collapses, so will its ability to support the human population. And so who's coming to the rescue once again as these final days draw nigh?

The Greys.

Today, these aliens need no description. By now, everyone knows what they look like, with those wraparound eyes and oversized heads. Their Mind is a collective mentality. No one individual is superior. And, according to Brown, they are in good standing with the Federation.

And, again, they have the technology to transcend Time and Space. "Although the Greys seem to be able to temporarily shift their presence

Grey Alien
"The rescuing cavalry"?

from subspace to physical space," Brown writes, "no data seems to suggest that ETs have the ability to defeat the speed-of-light limitation in the physical Universe without first leaving the physical Universe."

According to Brown, these Greys also know when someone (like a remote viewer) is watching them. And when they do not want that someone to have access to the information, "They can create a substitute signal that will either block the viewer's vision, or tailor the viewer's mind and experiences in such a way that he will better understand it. Such data can then only be interpreted symbolically."

Brown believes that the reports of humans being abducted and used against their will as incubators for genetically-engineered offspring (part-human and part-ET) may be for our own benefit. This genetic interbreeding with Mankind will make it easier for our species to survive the upcoming changes. It will be the Greys' gene pool which will help life on Earth to recover; otherwise, the human race would disappear.

"We must keep an open mind and not prejudge anything," Brown writes. "They [the aliens] are God's children, no less valuable than these we call human. We must work with them. They have to do with a greater evolutionary goal. When seen in this light, the Greys are less an invading army than once again a rescuing Cavalry."

Brown also notes that along with obtaining human gene samples, the Greys are also heavily involved in storing vegetation and animal genetic samples from the very environment that humans are so busy destroying. We will be grateful for their efforts in later years when we begin to rebuild this planet using these stored genetic stocks.

It also seems that some selected human beings will be transported (enraptured?) to a safe haven while the rest of humanity is left to slug it out back home. Where this safe haven will be is anybody's guess, but a subsequent viewing session by Brown showed this place to possibly be the Pleiades star system. He writes that he saw a "sense of maintaining a wide gene pool."

Obviously, Brown's remote viewing sessions were revealing that there is much more to the UFO phenomenon than simply flying saucers. It involves the genetic manipulation and ultimately the salvation of the human species. It also involves the dilemma of once again coming to the rescue of the underground Martians.

For one remote viewing session, Brown's set of "target coordinates" was God. Brown found that God is not a man sitting on a throne with a white beard and staff. He discovered that God is so great (in the sense of broad) that the human mind can only know parts at a time. It seems that God literally exists in fragmented form in everything—in life and matter—and that our ability to understand depends on our own level of what some call "God consciousness."

Brown writes: "There are galaxies, infinite diversity, all expanding. There is great joy, great joy in God's new existence. Great joy! It is as if God experiences joy in creating matter and life in his own substance, then living life through the experiences of species everywhere. Every living being is defined in terms of its ability to discover the relationship between the original God source and their own selves."

As far as human beings are concerned, there are two forms of life—physical and subspace—and we are composites of the two. Our physical forms (bodies) are temporary creations while our subspace selves (souls) are eternal.

Brown writes that his remote viewing experiences have shaken him to the core. "In only two years, all of the belief facade that structured my view of the world collapsed. I learned that we are not alone in the Universe, and that nonphysical beings share this dimensional reality with me."

Brown leaves us with some information regarding Scientific Remote Viewing, a path which consists of three distinct parts:

(1) Meditation. The biggest obstacle. "It is easier to tell people in our society that their blood pressure will improve with the practice of Transcendental Meditation than it is to tell them that they will soon become aware of their own souls."

(2) The Monroe Institute. A set of thirty-six audio tapes. "Robert Monroe has labeled his patented technology 'Hemi-sync.' Hemi-sync sounds put one frequency in one ear (for example, a 100-hertz tone) and another frequency only slightly different from the first in the other ear (say, a 104-hertz tone). The result is a very low frequency vibrato called a beat frequency. A beat frequency is not actually heard in the ears, but the mind can discern it. The brain itself creates it by blending the two separate audio frequencies. In this way, sound is used to cause an electrochemical reaction in the brain."

(3) Formal training in Scientific Remote Viewing. "SRV is a

procedure designed to extend the range of human perception beyond the immediate environment of time and space. It is necessary to learn how to control and direct the human consciousness. There are a number of former military officers who are now teaching the Army's version of remote viewing."

I tried reaching Brown for an interview, but he did not respond. He is presently suffering under his Comet Hale-Bopp fiasco, explained in the following question:

The mystery of comets has been a long-lasting one. Their tails always pointing away from the sun, no matter in which direction the comet is heading, these "dirty snowballs" have long been believed to be an omen of some kind. What we know for certain is that Comet Hale-Bopp was the third comet within three consecutive decades to pass within view of the naked eye on planet Earth: Comet Kohoutek (1973), which was barely visible to the naked eye, and a disappointment to many; Halley's Comet (1986), always deemed to be an harbinger of major news, and due to appear again in 2061;

(Comet Shoemaker-Levy [1994] could not be seen with the naked eye, but the "disrupted comet" of enormous asteroids gave Jupiter such a pummelling that astronomers called it "the single most important celestial event of the century.")

Comet Hale-Bopp (1997), however, has been called "the greatest comet of the century." It had a cone of ice twenty-five miles wide, was 120 million miles away, traveling at 93,000 mph, and dragging a tail of vapor 25 million miles long. The Heaven's Gate cult committed mass suicide in expectation that they were to meet up with a UFO following in the comet's tail. To do so, they had to shed their "vehicles," and thus their suicides.

Art Bell, of the nationally-syndicated radio talk show *Dreamland*, alleges that Brown, who claimed to have remote viewed the UFO in the comet's tail, perpetrated a fraud on the people by doctoring a photograph of the comet. The photo showed a bright but fake UFO trailing in its wake, which Bell subsequently showed on his web site. Dr. Brown, do you have any comments on this?

No doubt due to the implications of the question, Brown would not respond to correspondence.

I sought out Robert Monroe at the Monroe Institute for more information on the science of remote viewing and altering states of consciousness. Monroe's trilogy of books on out-of-body experiences, starting with his classic *Journeys Out Of The Body* (Doubleday, 1971), have a combined sales of one million copies, translated into twenty languages. Monroe wrote: "The greatest illusion is that Mankind has limitations."

Monroe died in 1995, but I was able to get in touch with "Skip" Atwater, Director of Research at the Monroe Institute. It turns out that Atwater had a couple of fascinating stories to tell about the U.S. Army's remote viewing program.

The first concerned Dr. Harold Puthoff, who, along with Russell Targ, originally eveloped the science of "trav-

"Skip" Atwater
(Courtesy of "Skip" Atwater)

eling clairvoyance" at Stanford Research Institute (SRI), a private think tank located in Menlo Park, California. Records supposedly show that the CIA sponsored the PSI research, which included investigations into ESP, astral projection, and psychokinesis. The remote viewing program experimented with clairvoyance ("the psychic seeing of things otherwise hidden for use in espionage").

According to Atwater, Puthoff was given an envelope in 1973 by a man named Pat Price, who showed up one day at SRI claiming that he could "remote view." The CIA took a subsequent interest in Price, who quickly gained a reputation as a man who could "see" anywhere in the world through his psychic powers. The envelope that Price gave Puthoff was said to list the geographical locations of four underground UFO bases situated around the globe. Price claimed to have remote viewed these bases on his own. The four bases were located at:

Mt. Perdido (Spain, near the Pyrennes). Price's description of the site included sensing a large artificial electromagnetic field, and a two-mile radius of detectors surrounding the base to prevent discovery;

Mt. Inyangani (Zimbabwe, north of South Africa). Price's remote viewing impressions of this base was that it seemed to be a maintenance and technical center; he observed lots of spare parts and equipment;

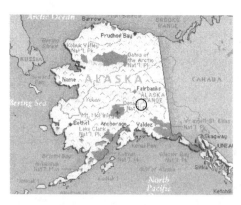

Mt. Hayes (Alaska). Price saw computer equipment and monitoring devices for "looking at things showing these bases were about to be discovered." A team of personnel would then be deployed to make sure that the activity would fail and the base would not be discovered;

Mt. Ziel (Northern Territory, Australia). Price's description of the site was that it had the feeling of a personnel area. He saw many different types of aliens there, and also saw contact between the aliens and *Homo sapiens* taking place there. Price also said that these aliens were capable of thought induction transfer, able to induce instant sleep through a remote hypnosis capability.

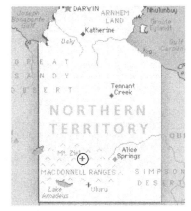

Atwater first got involved with SRI back in 1977 as an Intelligence Officer with the U.S. Army. As Operations Manager, it was his job to test and evaluate the skills of his military remote viewers. It was during this period that he came to work with Puthoff, and was given the envelope containing the locations of the UFO bases.

Atwater held onto it until the mid-eighties when, as a challenge to his team of remote viewers, he started giving the "geographic coordinates" of these underground bases to his officers. These highly-skilled officers, unaware of the locations to where they were being sent, and operating under the strictest set of protocols, began confirming to Atwater the strange activities of these "sites" and their ET overtones.

I found Atwater to be articulate and candid as he spoke by phone from his office at the Monroe Institute in Virginia. He's been with the Institute for twelve years now, and has worked with psychics for over twenty-two years. I asked him to tell more of what his remote viewers learned about these UFO bases.

"Their viewing information," replied Atwater, "revealed that these bases all seemed protected from discovery, they are mutually supportive in purpose, and they consist of very high technology. And that there were more of these bases located underwater. The good news is that the purpose of these sites seemed benign."

Could your team actually see the aliens?

"There was no report of actually seeing the alien beings, only of the bases themselves, and equipment."

Why would that be?

"There could be many reasons: a psychological blocking mechanism, for example."

Do you foresee contact with aliens soon?

"Apparently millions of people are having contact with the aliens on a personal basis. What you're asking about is an open contact, recognized by the Government, but I don't have an answer to that. I do think we are being prepared."

Have you had any UFO experiences?

"As a child, I must have seen a lot of UFOs because I have clear memories of sightings."

Some ex-military remote viewers claim that during the Persian Gulf War, they "saw" Saddam Hussein's soldiers igniting the Kuwaiti oil fires then releasing chemical and bacterial sprays into the billowing clouds of black smoke. Have you heard of this?

"No, I haven't. I was out of the military by then, and I went straight to the Monroe Institute."

You left the military in 1987. Do you believe that the military has proceeded with their remote viewing program, even though it's been officially disbanded?

"Yes. The original program was called 'Grill Flame' and the project officially ended with 'Stargate.' But I believe that there was telepathy research going on in the Government before 'Grill Flame,' and I'm sure that it still goes on today."

So the military must have confidence in the validity of

telepathy and remote viewing.

> "I believe that they have confidence in the validity of proven people. Just as in baseball, not all players are home run hitters, but you do get that occasional exceptional player."

Have you remote viewed?

> "No."

Then as Operations Manager, how would you know how to train remote viewers?

> "I consider myself to be extremely psychic. As a teenager, I had out-of-body experiences all of the time, so I was able to train my officers in what I knew, in my heart, was true."

A recent poll showed that most people would consider an out-of-body experience to be proof of an afterlife. How likely is it that the average person will have an out-of-body experience?

> "We all have out-of-body experiences every single night, when we are in an unconscious and deep delta sleep. The problem is not having one, but bringing it back to conscious experience."

And what do you think their impression would be if they were to bring it back to conscious experience?

> "When the average person does have a conscious out-of-body experience, it certainly has a very strong impact on them. They return knowing that they are more than a physical body, and they no longer fear death in any physical way."

Tell us what you know about Dr. Courtney Brown and his Comet Hale-Bopp predicament?

> "Courtney was trained in remote viewing so that he could interview remote viewers. As a result, when he sent his own team of viewers to trail the comet, he failed to exercise proper control status. By this, I mean that he front-loaded them by asking them leading

questions. Instead of allowing them to remote view blind, his questions allowed for analytical overlay and imagination. But I don't think that Brown purposefully created the ruse."

How did you come to meet Robert Monroe?

"I met him in 1977 when the Army first contacted Monroe. He was showing the ability to induce advanced states of consciousness. He was contracted to help train our officers to get into a receptive state. I found his Hemi-Sync technology quite effective."

For example?

"My first time under Monroe's control, I felt physically levitated from off the bed, then I traveled through a long tube until I arrived at the curved end, and just as I popped my head out—I was outside the tube and watching myself coming out of the tube. The instant lesson I learned there was that 'wherever you go, there you are.' I had traveled all that way to find that I was already there."

Considering your out-of-body experiences, how do you view the Creator of this Universe?

"I believe that we are mind, body, and spirit. The concept that I identify with is 'pantheism.' It's the belief that the cosmos and everything in it is Divine. We are all grounded in a common energy of shared Oneness. That's exactly how I feel. I consider myself to be a very spiritual guy."

After the interview, while reviewing my notes about remote viewing, I closed my eyes and projected my thoughts far away, and I found myself looking down upon my loved ones, seeing them smiling and laughing. Was my impression of them at that time a correct one? Were they happy? Or do we truly create our own reality—my mind only imagining that they were smiling and laughing?

Or was it my own mind that was smiling and laughing?

The Universe is so vast with possibilities, it's hard to know. And now with a technology like remote viewing, I guess we can run but we can no longer hide. State secrets and personal secrets will no longer be confidential. We will be like windows. Eyes could be watching us. No one can be comfortable. (Rumor already has it that a remote viewer who transports himself to the White House will not get in. He will be met outside by psychic security guards, America's best ESPs.)

Will this technology be used for good or evil? As Atwater might put it, it's in the hands of the beholder.

As for those Martians living underground, Dr. Brown, there isn't a soul on Earth who wouldn't sympathize with them. I half-suspect there are many of us up here who would move underground with them if we could. Those Martians below ground don't know what they're missing.

Or maybe they do.

Cosmic Voyage: A Scientific Discovery of Extraterrestrials Visiting Earth
(Dutton Books, 1996)
Dr. Courtney Brown

For more information on Hemi-Sync, write to:
The Monroe Institute
62 Robert Mt. Road
Faber, Virginia 22938

www.monroeinstitute.org

Chapter Four

The Time Bandit

An electronics whiz

discovers that he's

lived a double life

The Government thought they'd

brainwashed the project

out of him, but –

They didn't – and now he writes

We've broken the Time Barrier

The Time Bandit

Montauk Point is the easternmost end of Long Island, known to most New Yorkers for its landmark lighthouse. It is also home to a derelict Air Force Base, decommissioned in 1969, but subsequently reopened, supposedly without the sanction of the U.S. Government. Financing for the base is a mystery, as no funding can be traced to either the Government or the military. Thus begins the mystery. The secrecy of the operation has prompted legends, but to get to the end, we must first go back to the beginning.

That would be when Preston Nichols, described as "amazingly brilliant" in the field of electronics and considered a specialist in radar technology, went to work for an unnamed but well-known Long Island defense contractor in 1971. He had obtained a grant to study mental telepathy and to determine whether or not it existed. (His research eventually led him to believe that telepathy did indeed exist, and that telepathic communication operated on principles that are strikingly familiar to that of radio waves.)

One day in 1974, while monitoring his psychics, Nichols noticed that every day, at the same hour, persistent radio waves were interfering with their ability to transmit their thoughts.

He investigated and discovered that it was a 410-420 megahertz frequency jamming the airwaves, preventing his psychics from thinking effectively.

(Courtesy of Sky Books)

Fixing an antenna to the roof of his car, Nichols traced the radio signal to Long Island, where the frequency was coming from a large antenna on the Montauk Air Force Base. The base was active, and he could see that they were running an old World War II radar system known as "Sage Radar," but other than that, security was tight and he was kept outside the gates. And that was the end of it until 1984 when a friend informed him that the base was now closed and abandoned.

Nichols went out and found the place deserted. He also found electronics debris strewn everywhere, and he started buying up the abandoned equipment, although no one in the Government would officially say who was selling the equipment.

During his scavenging, Nichols met a homeless man living on the base. The man told him how a big top-secret experiment had taken place there a year earlier, then everything went crazy when a big beast appeared and frightened everyone away. The derelict also told Nichols that he recognized him as one of his bosses on the project. Nichols had no idea what the man was talking about, so he brought his psychics out to do a reading on the base. Their conclusions were that mind control had been the main focus of the experiments there, and that there had been some kind of a vicious beast running amok.

Nichols talked to the town citizens of Montauk, and he began hearing tales of how it had once snowed there in the middle of August, and of how hurricane winds would often appear out of nowhere. Strangest of all were the stories of how on occasion animals would come into town and crash through windows as if crazed.

"I was also being recognized by people I didn't know," writes Nichols. "Obviously I had severe memory blocks while a full set of normal memories were telling me where I'd been. I must have been existing on two separate time tracks. I had lived an entire second career here that I knew nothing about."

Nichols was soon to discover much more.

That day came in 1990, when he was reconstructing a

Preston Nichols
(Courtesy of Sky Books)

Delta T antenna, a piece of equipment that he had bought from the Montauk base. According to Nichols, a Delta T antenna is an octahedronal antenna designed to shift time zones by bending time: "The more soldering I did, the more the time functions were causing my mind to shift. Then, one day—bang!—the whole memory line blew open for me. This was my memory breakthrough. I was now sure that I had been living two separate existences."

By June of 1990, all his key memories had come back, and he began asking questions. One month later, after two decades with the defense firm, he was laid off. "I can't even talk about it," Nichols writes. "It is Top Secret. I'm bound not to mention it for thirty years because of an agreement I signed when I went to work for the defense firm. However, I didn't sign a single thing regarding the activities of the Montauk Project."

Despite his brainwashing, and threats to silence him,

Nichols survived to tell his tale in his book *The Montauk Project*, believing it is in the best interest of all to tell his story. He believes that he worked on what was officially known as "Project Phoenix," the culmination, so to speak, of "Project Rainbow," an experiment in invisibility begun back in 1943. Since that story of The Philadelphia Experiment has already been written up extensively, here is a brief synopsis:

The Philadelphia Experiment was where the USS Eldridge, a fully-manned destroyer, actually disappeared while the Navy was conducting radar invisibility experiments. While the object of the experiment was to simply make the ship undetectable to radar, it had a totally unexpected result, and disastrous side effects for the crewmen involved.

The ship was rendered invisible, then was seen to reappear in Norfolk, Virginia, hundreds of miles away, before reappearing back into its original berth in the Philadelphia Naval Yard minutes later. The sailors had been transported out of this dimension upon being rendered invisible, and when they returned, some of the crew had vanished, some were embedded into the bulkhead of the ship itself, and those found walking were in a complete state of disorientation and absolute horror. Some of them claimed that they had entered into another realm and talked to strange aliens.

Nichols believes that the experiment accidentally ripped a hole in the Space-Time fabric, and it was soon after this that UFOs began entering into our realm. At first, the military referred to them as "flying unknowns," but for some reason the abbreviation "F.U." didn't stick.

This invisibility experiment was supposedly hatched at the Institute of Advanced Study, located on the grounds of Princeton University, New Jersey. It had a very small faculty, including Albert Einstein and Nikola Tesla, famed inventor and known as a "Father of Radio." The faculty did no teaching. The Institute's "students" were so expert in their fields that they presumably knew all of the facts involved. They were there to pursue their theoretical research, and if they stumbled upon a puzzle, they could take the conundrum to one of their faculty advisors, who would help them work on a solution.

The Institute had several top-secret defense-oriented projects going on during WWII, improbable projects such as attempting to split the atom ("indivisible"), and trying to establish anti-gravity. During the war years, America was reaching for aid in every direction it could.

At the same time, Einstein was busy trying to unify his Unified Field Theory. Today, it still remains an unfinished theory about gravity and electromagnetism, but it became the theoretical basis for the Navy's invisibility experiments. It also paved the way for the splitting of the atom, ushering in the Atomic Age.

Einstein's theories contributed to The Philadelphia Experiment, but the nuts-and-bolts of the project was headed by Dr. John von Neumann, the theoretical physicist who built the first vacuum tube computer at Princeton University. He was said to have the unique ability to take abstract theories and apply them to physical situations: That is, he served as a bridge between Einstein and the technical engineers.

When one of the projects succeeded in splitting the atom (the atomic test explosion at Alamogordo, New Mexico, being a success), all other projects were then suspended until the end of the war when they would take another look at them. After the war, the invisibility project was resumed under the name "Project Phoenix." Dr. von Neumann led the team as they continued their investigation into the invisibility phenomena encountered by the USS Eldridge.

Einstein's Unified Field Theory paved the way for the splitting of the atom, ushering in the Atomic Age (Courtesy of David Childress)

The Philadelphia Experiment had dissolved the biological structure of the crewmen in such a way that when they came back, in some cases, they were reassembled beyond recognition. So a massive human factor study was begun at Brookhaven Labs on Long Island, where they spent ten years working on why human beings had trouble with the electromagnetic fields that shifted them through different places and times.

The project discovered that the extensive degaussing coils placed around the hull of the USS Eldridge, attempting to demagnetize the hull so that the ship would not trip underwater mines, also created a soloton (a self-contained electromagnetic field) around the ship. According to Nichols, this created a vacuum, or a "bubble reality." When the ship was demagnetized, the particles of matter became waves, and the entire ship and crew disappeared. It created stealth by isolating the ship within a "bottle effect." Nichols believes that this "bottle effect" is the forerunner of today's stealth technology.

The problem faced by "Phoenix Project" was how to send human beings into this "bottle effect" and bring them back out without harm. Dr. von Neumann died in 1957, but the project continued until it was completed in 1967. A final report was then prepared by the Navy and presented to Congress, who had thus far funded the project.

"Congress was told that the consciousness of man could definitely be affected by electromagnetics," writes Nichols. "In addition, they were advised that it was possible to develop equipment that could literally change the way a person thinks."

Congress said no to further funding. They were concerned that this technology could fall into the wrong hands. Word was given to disband the program, and "Project Phoenix" came to an halt.

So Brookhaven Labs looked elsewhere for funding. Smoke trails say that they went directly to the U.S. military and told them of this fantastic new technology they were developing, based upon frequencies, and designed to make the enemy surrender at the flick of a switch. (This brings to mind images of the Iraqi soldiers surrendering en masse during the Persian Gulf War, the same fierce fighters who had fought an eight-year-long Holy War against Iran.)

Although the financing is still shrouded in mystery, by the 1970s operations at Montauk Point AFB were back underway. The underwriting of the project appears to have been totally private, which is precisely why Nichols broke his silence and wrote this book. "This book is discussing a project which should never have been activated in the first place. Its only purpose was for controlling minds."

The project began looking into "psychotronics," a science whereby one can tune into a specific frequency and snare it, thereby also snaring an individual and jamming his thoughts. This would make the individual change accordingly. For this, they required a huge radiosonde that would operate at around 425 to 450 megahertz. From earlier research, it had been discovered that this was the "window frequency" for getting into the human consciousness. A high-powered radar device was needed, and the Montauk AFB had just what they were looking for, the old WWII Sage Radar reflector, nearly as large as a football field.

This was where Nichols believes that he was first drawn into the project as a radar specialist with the defense firm. His continued investigation would ultimately reveal his role as one of the technical directors of the project.

It was during this time that they discovered that frequency hopping—randomly shifting to any of five frequencies being fed through the transmitter—was the key to bending time. They also discovered that by changing the frequency and the pulse, they could change the general way people were thinking, which was what they were looking for.

The project involved having someone sit in the "chair" in an isolated building, and the huge Sage Radar reflected down upon the building. The transmitter would blast out gigawatts of power down onto the building and the person sitting in the chair. At 425-450 MHz of radio frequency power, they found they had a window into the human mind and were able to influence brain waves.

Nichols relates that at this point in the project, they were

Montauk AFB - where the Montauk Project did their mind control experiments on vacationing servicemen (Courtesy of Sky Books)

only interested in monitoring people and changing their moods. It was not important how they changed but the fact that they changed. Military personnel on R&R at the Montauk base were used as guinea pigs as the project directors would turn the huge Sage Radar down upon them and do their mind control experiments on the vacationing servicemen.

The Montauk chair in the isolated building was surrounded by Delta T Coils similar to the ones placed around the USS Eldridge. The chair was connected to radio receivers studded with crystals that sent the individual's thoughts out through a giant transmitter. The theory was that the person sitting in the chair could transmit an alternate reality. According to Nichols, the chair and the way they used it in the movie *Total Recall* is strikingly similar to the Montauk chair.

The person usually sitting in this chair was a man named Duncan Cameron, said to be an extremely operational psychic. Cameron claims that in his past life, he and his brother had served as crew members aboard the USS Eldridge during The Philadelphia Experiment back in 1943. He believes that he and his brother jumped overboard in hopes of escaping the electromagnetic field of the ship as they were being thrust into a time vortex.

"Over the years," writes Nichols, "the Montauk researchers perfected their mind control techniques. It eventually got to the point where a psychic's thought could be amplified with hardware into a virtual creation of matter. Duncan could sit in the chair, concentrate on a solid object—and it would precipitate out of the ether! Often, it would be only visible and not solid to the touch, like a ghost."

The project also experimented with putting thoughts into other people's heads, and Cameron was able to push his mind so far into the mind of another that he could control that person's thoughts and make them do what he wanted.

After three decades of secret research, these mind control techniques were fully developed. By 1981, everything was aligned and ready to function, and all unnecessary personnel were removed from the project. Cameron stayed on as the psychic in the chair who made the whole operation work, and all project directors, including Nichols, stayed on.

Cameron was in the chair ninety percent of the time, although there were other psychics too. The huge Sage Radar was angled down upon the building, blasting out its frequency upon Cameron as he sat in the chair. He would concentrate on an opening in time, and a "hole," or time portal, would appear. Then a technician, or another "volunteer," would walk into the vortex.

As to the vortex, Nichols writes: "Those who traveled through the vortex described it as a peculiar spiral tunnel that was lit. The tunnel resembled a corkscrew with an effect similar to lit bulbs. It was not a straight tunnel but twisted and took turns until you'd come out the other end. There, you would meet somebody or do something. Many alien encounters were reported. However, if they lost power during the operation, you'd be lost somewhere in hyperspace (defined as space which exceeds the boundaries of

The Vortex Tunnel
(Courtesy of Sky Books)

three dimensions). Many people were lost in this vortex."

Then on Aug. 12, 1983, forty years to the day after the Philadelphia Experiment, the Montauk Project effectively ripped a hole in the Space-Time fabric, and the USS Eldridge appeared through the portal of the vortex. They had locked up with the ship. It was at this point that Cameron from 1943 could be seen standing on the deck of the ship with his brother. Cameron of 1983 was unable to see himself, but the technicians could. They felt that Natural Laws were being violated, and everyone involved felt uncomfortable.

That's when someone inside the project (perhaps Nichols himself?) activated a contingency program in Cameron. Cameron imagined a giant beast, unleashed it from his subconscious, and it ran amok outside on the base. It literally destroyed the project, eating anything it could, smashing everything in sight.

"Many people saw it," writes Nichols, "but almost everyone describes a different beast. Fright does strange things to people, and no one was sure of what the exact physical constitution of this monster was, but they all agreed that it was big, hairy and nasty."

The project directors turned off the generators, but the power remained on, and the Beast outside kept on the rampage. With an acetylene torch, they cut every wire in two, but the Beast continued to exist and destroy. Finally, they used the torch to cut apart the transmitter itself until ultimately the Beast faded back into the ether.

But the Beast had done its job and frightened everyone into stopping the project. The entire Montauk base virtually emptied, and the personnel were rounded up, debriefed and brainwashed, including Nichols. The air shafts and entrances leading to the underground facilities were supposedly filled with cement.

But time travel had just taken a huge step.

As time passed, the brainwashed memories of the project slowly returned to Nichols, although some of the aspects of his involvement remain hidden to this day. He writes: "This project exploited individuals and caused untold misery. It could easily be considered to be the work of dark forces, perpetrated by individuals who were not acting within their legal bounds of the law. There was a sinister energy about the Montauk Project."

Peter Moon, the writer who stumbled across Nichols' story and persuaded him to put it into print, has this to say about his impressions of the Montauk Project: "I don't even know if any of this information is true. Hard facts about Montauk are difficult to obtain. If the story isn't true, I thought it better than any science fiction that I'd ever read. But if it is true, it's obvious to me what the whole importance is behind the entire Montauk story. It could be the opportunity to regain our inheritance. The Age of Aquarius has mandated that we will recover the lost knowledge of millennia."

Cameron, who sat in the Montauk chair while being bombarded with high frequencies, has apparently suffered significant brain impairment and tissue damage. How many casualties were actually involved in the whole project is unknown, but Nichols estimates the body count was probably high.

Still, the one question remains: Who was behind the funding the Montauk Project?

Today, the entirety of Montauk Point, including the Air Force base and the Montauk Point Lighthouse (originally commissioned by George Washington) is a New York State Park. It is a popular tourist attraction, although entrance onto the base is "mostly illegal." Supposedly, the underground tunnels are still there, miles in length, leading through the underground testing facility. Various cats roam the area, and it's said that if you follow the cats before a rainstorm, they will lead you to the underground tunnels.

Coincidentally enough, Montauk Point was named for the North American Indian spirit guide "Manatu" – a shape shifter and time traveler.

The USS Eldridge was sold to the Greek Navy, who later uncovered the log books and found that everything before

January of 1944 had been omitted from the records.

Since 1995, there have been virtually no transmissions out of Montauk AFB.

Together, Moon and Nichols wrote an absorbing account of this experiment in their book *The Montauk Project*, eventually developing it into a trilogy of books as they pieced together parts of the Montauk puzzle.

Speaking by phone from New York City, Moon proved to be an intensely-driven seeker in his search for the Truth, having authored five books concerning the Montauk mystery. My first question to him was to ask what he hoped to accomplish by writing about the elusive Montauk Project.

"To enlighten Mankind and share a fascinating story," Moon replied. "And hopefully, give people a sense of their own self-determinism in creating their own reality."

And what do you believe is the biggest misconception that people hold about reality and life?

"They readily accept all data as truth. They need to be more discriminating."

You have also written at length about Secret Societies, especially in reference to those who were behind the funding of the Montauk Project. How have these "secret societies" managed to stay secret for so long?

"The subject is so vast, complex, hidden, that I couldn't give more than a brief rendition here. They are a secret society within a secret society within a secret society. That's the whole secret. If we knew where the 'control zone' was, they wouldn't be a secret any more."

In my review, I neglected to state your association with L. Ron Hubbard, a former Naval Intelligence officer who went on to found Scientology ("to know in the deepest sense"). His organization has a worldwide following based upon his principles known as Dianetics. You once worked as Hubbard's assistant, and your description of his intellectual and psychic brilliance was certainly intriguing. Care to elaborate on this fascinating mind?

> "I might one day write a book on it. It would take a book to describe the whole phenomenon. But he was a genius, and the attacks against him are completely unfounded. As William Burroughs once put it: The problem is that you can't criticize something without being a part of the movement. You have to participate on some level. Hubbard's life was dedicated to raising the consciousness of humanity. His attackers do not have equal power. They must show us something better."

Are you still involved with Scientology?

> "I have no affiliation with them today, but it still holds spiritual truths for me."

In Book III of the Montauk Project trilogy, you wrote about The Hundredth Monkey Effect, which is the supposition that if a certain percentage of the monkey population learns something, the function will automatically telepath to all similar monkeys on the planet, even those who are isolated on an island. The critical monkey who bridges the gap is referred to as "The Hundredth Monkey."

You believe that the mathematics show that if only ten percent of the human beings on this planet can become conscious of the original Time Line (God), then all beings will follow suit. When this happens, the Great Transition will take place. How probable is this?

> "You can see examples of it in the world today. When you think of someone, like a movie star, for instance, it's telepathic. If enough people think of him or her, the masses pick up on the trend, because thought rules."

I told Moon of my dream about Lennon and McCartney and

myself playing our guitars by a river, and that upon awakening, how sorry I felt for having intruded upon their consciousness, and I wondered how many thousands of fans intruded upon John and Paul in their dreams. Moon laughed.

"Exactly. They're an awareness that reaches almost everybody."

You and Nichols have both written about your UFO experiences. Have you any new UFO sightings to report?

"I have nothing new to add. I'm not a UFO junkie. I'm more interested in what is happening in terms of mass consciousness. I don't even know if I believe in the End Time. It's too apocalyptic for me. I think it's all an outward manifestation of the changes taking place in our mass consciousness."

In 1996, TWA Flight 800 took off from a New York airport. Witnesses have said that they saw a streak of light shoot up from Long Island, followed by an explosion before the passenger plane disintegrated in midair. I couldn't help but note that Montauk AFB is located at Long Island.

"The rumor in my circle has it that it was the particle accelerator at Brookhaven Labs on the Montauk Point, part of the SDI [Strategic Defense Initiative] program. The plane was passing in the vicinity of a military exercise where a heat-generated target was being pursued, but something malfunctioned. The beam was accidentally fired up from the ground, hitting the deactivated missile, and activating it. The heat-seeking missile passed through the hull of the plane, destroying it, and leaving no trace of itself. The Government can't investigate this too deeply because it's a part of the supposedly defunct Star Wars system."

And what about Duncan Cameron, the psychic in the Montauk chair, bombarded with gigawatts of power?

"Duncan is an individual who has been..."
[Long silence.]

Used and abused?

"Yes. Duncan is an individual who has been used and abused. He now works as a carpenter in a regular life, trying to make ends meet. I've been encouraging him to write a book, if only for therapeutic reasons."

Where is Peter Moon today as a result of becoming involved in the Montauk story?

"The Montauk story proved to be a life-transforming vehicle for me. It has many esoteric meanings in order to help us understand the Light. I first stumbled upon Preston Nichols when I was looking to market one of his inventions, but his story has turned out to be a very apt vehicle for me to explore the Light."

In light of all this, what is your belief about God?

"To me, God is a name for the creative principle of the Universe. God means Creation."

Moon gave me Nichols' phone number, and I was able to speak to Nichols in New York. I found him to be guarded and thoughtful in how he perceives the Montauk situation to be. I told him how after reading his book describing all of this advanced technology, the last line of his book read: "There is still nothing that will replace a man working at a bench and trying out a circuit." That presented a powerful image of artistry to me.

"The best discoveries are made by the individual," replied Nichols, "because they are usually serendipitous. When you want to delve deeply into something, you're much better off trying it out alone at a bench."

I titled your review "The Time Bandit," although it was they, the project funders, who stole time from you. Are you outraged by that theft?

> "Yes and no. They have made restitution for
> it. That's about all I can say on it."

Were you harassed by the Intelligence communities for
your participation in revealing the Montauk story?

> "In the beginning I was. Now it's settled
> down."

I found your suggestion that the Cross has long been a symbol of conquering Time and Space to be very interesting,
especially in this Age of Christ.

> "When a second Time Line is created, which
> we created ourselves when we separated
> from God, the Original Time Line, it's
> inevitable they will once again cross. The
> Cross is basically the representation of the
> intersection where our Time Line crosses the
> Creator's."

And what is your impression of this Creator?

> "I have never seen an inkling of God in my
> work, but there's some sort of Intelligence
> out there. There's too much order in the
> Universe not to have a Creator. The Christ
> figure is a good representation."

So, Mr. Nichols, have you ever time traveled?

> "Yes. I believe it was through the portal at
> Montauk, though I can scarcely remember it.
> But one day in 1995, there was a forest fire
> in the Pine Barrens on Montauk Island. I was
> at home watching the newscasts, and they
> were showing the 'hot shots' in there putting
> out the fire. They had an odd symbol on
> their T-shirts, a triangle with a second trian-
> gle going into the side of it. I realized they
> weren't firefighters, they were paramilitary.
> Then I saw myself on TV, fighting the fire and
> wearing one of the T-shirts. So I went down
> there, and I approached myself. He ran away

and I got sick, but by that time I saw that the cause of the fire was a crashed UFO.

"It was later, through hypnosis, that I recalled entering through the Montauk vortex, which was probably sometime around 1972, and going to fight the fire of 1995. I recognized many of the other firefighters there, too. I later learned that the 'Delta' emblem on their T-shirts was actually a stylized UFO grouping, and that the Delta Force is in reality a UFO recovery team. A number of us making up this Delta team were time travelers, but why they had us there, I have no idea."

The alien connection played a heavy part in the Montauk experiments. You wrote that you helped to "shoot down" a UFO when you worked for the defense firm. You did this by jamming its drive with the appropriate frequencies, which caused the saucer to became unstable: "We watched it fluttering and wobbling and making a strange whiny noise as it went down into the ocean. There was a large splash and a thud. The incident is known as the Moriches Bay UFO crash." Do you believe that the U.S. Government is preparing to do battle with extraterrestrials?

"It's happening right now. We're at war with somebody, be it ETs, other beings on this planet, or other dimensions on this planet, maybe even our own futures."

Do you believe these ETs to be friendly?

"Some are friendly, some are not. Some look human, and some do not. That's the Government's dilemma. Imagine this scenario: A UFO crashes in Roswell and you find human body parts soaking in liquid nitrogen. How do you tell the public that this alien group, in this advanced craft, from you don't know where, is here harvesting Mankind,

using the human race for food, genetics, slavery—whatever. What kind of message can
you tell them?"

At the conclusion of the Nichols interview, I picked up my
notes and found that Moon had supplied me with names and
phone numbers to aid me in my UFO research. I appreciated
his generosity, but Moon makes a living on a path that helps
him to explore consciousness, so his generosity is being
rewarded.

The human mind is a powerful thing, and to study it is to
search for meaning in a vast puzzling universe. And surely, in
our search through space, a time machine would be high on
the wish list. (Although I've heard tell that once you return
from the future, things will never be the same as they were.)

And I smiled when I recalled telling Moon about how long
the waiting list was for his books at the library, and he respond-
ed, "Tell the library to buy more books!"

Unfortunately, Mr. Moon, having the L.A. library system pur-
chase more books will not solve this world's dilemma. Libraries
are seldom packed. And if time travel is already a reality, it'll
arrive in our homes soon enough. As for the individual, it still
ultimately comes down to: What is the destiny of human consciousness after death?

Death will be the ultimate time travel, and then, of course,
we won't need to read any more books.

The Montauk Trilogy (Sky Books):
The Montauk Project (1992)
Montauk Revisited (1994)
Pyramids of Montauk (1995)
         Preston Nichols and Peter Moon

For a listing of books and tapes, write to:
         Sky Books
         Box 769
         Westbury, New York 11590

         email: skybooks@yahoo.com

Chapter Five

The Man
of Aquarius

As a child – he encountered

a multidimensional being

As a young man – a Spirit Guide

inspired him to write a book

Now he writes of channelers

who say to get ready

Earth's vibrations

are about to change

The Man
of Aquarius

"The UFO phenomenon is a deluge, not a delusion."

Bold words, but they come from the Man of Aquarius, a writer who has spent his career investigating life's greatest mysteries. Brad Steiger's numerous books, which run the gamut from American Indian Medicine to Guardian Angels to the Mysteries of Animal Intelligence, compels one to redefine the term "cult writer." If terrain is any indication, this man is a true spiritual explorer. It is doubtful that anyone has written more books on the paranormal than Steiger.

Why the passion?

He's heard the word. His book *The Fellowship* is about "channelers," men and women who claim to be receiving communications from Higher Intelligences. These New Age prophets say that humankind is facing a Great Purification.

Steiger writes: "These channelers receive their advice in much the same way as the Old Testament prophets who heard their voices and imparted their messages. However, the mystery still remains: Who are these beings who have been communicating with humankind since his earliest days?"

Despite having written more than one hundred books covering the spiritual realm, Steiger says that it is still impossible

(Courtesy of Ivy Books)

to offer a universally acceptable answer to the question of the true identity of these Higher Intelligences. On the bright side, they may be God's angels coming to down gather the elect as promised in Psalm 68:17: "The chariots of God are twenty thousand, even thousands of angels; the Lord is among them." Steiger points out that in Scripture, the term "angel" is used to designated a messenger sent to accomplish a mission; not a god, but a created being.

Then, of course, there's the flip side of the picture: They could be the dreaded "chariots of Satan," also warned against in Scripture, which tells how God's angels divided themselves into two vast hosts, those obedient to God, and those who were the Fallen Angels, loyal to Satan and known as demons. These angelic ranks were formed long before humankind was scooped from the dust of the Earth.

But there is also a third possibility. New Age channelers are telling us that these Higher Intelligences just may be our cosmic ancestors. The Old Testament refers to the Creator of humankind in the plural *Elohim* ("Those who came from the sky"). The line in Genesis 1:26 reads: "Let *us* make man in *our* image." These Elohim created a being they called *adamah* (Earthling).

Steiger writes: "In a manner similar to Pygmalion, who created a statue so beautiful that he fell in love with it, the Elohim found the results of their laboratory DNA artistry so compelling irresistible that 'it came to pass that the sons of God saw the daughters of men that they were fair; and they took them wives of all which they chose' (Gen. 6:2)."

Steiger has made an occupation of trying to bring together all of the psychological and biological and spiritual implications of the impending New Age. A summary of his body of work shows that life consists of many more dimensions than we realize. His books tell of a potentially richer Universe of beings than most of us are bold enough to believe.

"And it came to pass that the sons of gods saw the daughters of men that they were fair, and they took them wives of all which they chose."

"*Homo sapiens* view the Universe through a slender speck of the visual spectrum," writes Steiger. "We are looking out of our own world through a tiny crack and, perhaps arrogantly, proclaiming the dimensions of being. But if one accepts one God-Intelligence for the Universe, why should his Divine Handiwork not manifest itself wherever it chooses?"

Steiger has been studying channelers since 1967, and has seen a definite increase in these angelic/space contacts taking place around the world. With their emphasis upon spiritual teachings, he believes these UFO prophets are bringing God physically to the Earth by creating a whole new blend of science and religion, one more applicable to modern humankind.

Steiger has found their channeled messages to be constant and twofold. First and foremost, as these contacts themselves suggest, we are not alone in the Universe. And the overriding second message is that humankind is about to become part of a larger community of intelligences. But if humans do not shape up spiritually, then heavy times are upon us. Of course, the question then arises: If these Higher Intelligences are so concerned about us, why don't they help us outright?

Steiger writes: "These New Age channelers tell us that if help is given to the planet at this stage, it would absolutely be a worthless gesture. It might temporarily alleviate certain problems, but it would not alleviate the conditions that led to the problems. At any time, the human race has total freedom to build itself into any level it wants, or to destroy itself."

But, as Steiger points out, the word apocalypse means "to reveal." He believes that it will not be the terrible day of damnation we imagine, but rather the beginning of the Final Hours of the old age. The word horoscope means "that which looks at the hour," and New Agers say our horoscope reads that hour is at hand.

So who are these Higher Intelligences coming to assist us in our progression, and where do they come from?

On a clear night, you can see 4500 stars with the naked eye. With binoculars, you can see 6000 stars, and through a three-inch telescope, one-half million stars come into view. Far out in space, but within view of the naked eye, is a bright cluster of stars known as the Pleiades, classically referred as the "Seven Sisters." In Greek mythology, these seven sisters were the daughters of Atlas, who upholds the earth. These stars belong to the constellation we know as Taurus, four hundred light years away from our sun.

Steiger believes that all signs seem to point to these "Seven Sisters" as the source of our seed and our creation. Every civilization on Earth has some kind of a legend built around an experience with these "Seven Sisters." Even Devils Tower (Wyoming), seen in the film *Close Encounters of The Third Kind*, has an American Indian legend about the Pleiades connected with it. For decades now, scientists have speculated that if intelligent life did exist elsewhere in the Universe, the Pleiades would be one of the more likely candidates.

Many UFOlogists believe that the Pleiadeans are possibly

slightly out of dimension to us, and a bit higher in frequency, but from the same time reference that we are. Steiger has also come to suspect that what we have been labeling "spaceships" may actually be a form of a higher intelligence themselves rather than a nuts-and-bolts vehicle, only partially physical and partly ethereal at the same time. When in motion, they seem to become "living flames in flight."

Devils Tower, Wyoming
America's first national monument, and an impressive sight from all directions
(Courtesy of Wyoming Division of Tourism)

It's said, however, that in order to see these ethereal vehicles, belief is important. There is a story that tells how when Columbus's expedition landed in the West Indies, the natives, a canoe culture for centuries, were unable to see the huge ships anchored in their bay. It took their shamans to finally convince the villagers that the foreigners had indeed arrived in something; namely, in those huge ships out there. The natives referred to the newcomers as "men from heaven." Even today, it's believed that people often cannot see UFOs because of their own disbelief.

Throughout Biblical Scriptures, however, one caution is given to humankind concerning these angelic beings: We are not to worship them. They may be more advanced than us, spiritually and scientifically, but it is their moral obligation to assist those creatures who are evolving in a similar direction as themselves, and they are not to be adored.

So does the human species get saved?

The message of *The Fellowship* is that portions of humankind will attain a new consciousness, a new state of awareness, through a harmonic resonance. These channelers agree with the Pythagorean theory of creation, that sounds create our Universe. Each physical body is a state of vibration, invisible atoms vibrating into visibility. Scripture teaches that it was Logos—The Word—that first spoke and made these atoms resonate, thus creating matter.

What this boils down to is that the fundamental building block of everything that we consider to be real in this Universe breaks down into simple light. We as a species are literally "light beings" (hue-man).

These New Age prophets tell us that Earth's natural vibrational level is about to be stepped up. Humankind stands on the precipice of a quantum leap forward—on both a biological and a spiritual level. We must individually start thinking positively to assist in raising ourselves to these higher levels of vibration. Those who want to make it, will, and those who don't, won't.

This is the "I AM" of the New Age: "If thine eye be single, then thy whole body shall be full of light." When "hue-man" becomes fully stabilized, True Illumination will take place, and the body will begin to function with its full powers. Individuals will resonate with a higher octave and will graduate into the fourth dimensional frequency.

The word religion will not be applicable here because it means "reunification" with God, and at this point humans will realize that they are God, as is a tree, or an animal, or the sky. If God is all things, then everything is God.

Steiger's spiritual journey and discoveries have been clearly chronicled in his writings. He's prolific, and writes unabashedly about our being on the brink of a tremendous breakthrough. He believes that New Age man—Transformed Man—will make it through to a new world and a spiritually sane existence.

Steiger writes: "Today we are in the dark womb of Nativity called Earth. As we emerge from this womb to cry out into the new light of day, which the Space Brothers define as Christ consciousness, we will see that we have just begun to live, to grow, to understand."

People often approach Steiger at his lectures and seminars to thank him for the inspiration that his books have given them, an inspiration they find lacking in organized religions. Steiger describes his readers as people disenchanted with religion but not with God. He took the time to answer my questions at length, speaking on tape and sending me the cassette.

Brad Steiger
(Courtesy of Brad Steiger)

Mr. Steiger, in *The Fellowship*, you wrote about a Dr. Fred Bell, former NASA scientist and Rockwell employee. Bell claims to be the channeler of a spacewoman named Semjase. At last word, Semjase was helping him with his science projects duplicating Pleiadean technology. He was convinced that his anti-pollution device was most important because the pollution in our atmosphere is causing the pollution in our minds. This leads me to ask: Whatever happened to Fred Bell and his inventions?

"He's still at it," replied Steiger. "I haven't heard from him personally now for years, but I hear about him through mutual friends. He's working on his big time travel machine now."

And why would the Space People pick out one individual named Fred (nothing personal to Dr. Bell) and help him build a piece of technology, as opposed to giving it to all of humankind outright?

"Well, of course, they don't just pick out someone, whatever this Intelligence is, what-

ever this Creative Impulse is. And the one
thing I've said in books like *Divine Fire* and
so forth is that this [channeling] phenomenon is worldwide, and that these entities are,
um...I hate to say manipulating, but maybe
guiding or, and/or, manipulating us.
Throughout history they've been choosing
sensitive vehicles through which to channel
their knowledge, which in turn can be
shared with the masses."

Project Blue Book (Ballantine Books, 1976) is a compila-
tion of reports which was edited by Steiger. "Project Blue
Book" was an Air Force study begun in 1952 in response to the
increasing number of UFO sightings. A self-described "exercise
in charting a phenomenon," the project charted the UFO phenomenon until the late '60s when the project was suddenly
discontinued. For the most part, critics agree that the study
produced satisfactory explanations of most of the 13,000 sightings.

The "Committee to Review Project Blue Book" submitted
two conclusions: (1) "There appears to be no verified and fully
satisfactory evidence of any case that is clearly outside the
framework of presently known science and technology." (2)
"There are no indications that the phenomena reported are a
threat to the USA or, as far as we know, the rest of the world."

It's a conclusion intriguing for its noncommittedness, and I
remember reading *Project Blue Book* when it first came out
and believing it to be a whitewash. Was this writer telling it the
way it is? Or was he being a mouthpiece for the party line?
Now that I have the editor's ear, I have two questions: Did the
military believe the whitewash they were handing you? And
did you?

"Your remark—'A conclusion intriguing for
its noncommittedness'—is true, but yet as a
historical record, 'Project Blue Book' is
extremely valuable. I think it's dramatic to

say 'the party line' and 'a whitewash.' I think all this has been grossly exaggerated. I think that most of the military is as confused as anyone else. And certainly those who worked on 'Project Blue Book.' Oh yes, there may have been some cover-ups here and there, but as I said, there was no 'whitewash.'

"Did I believe the whitewash they were handing me? I saw it as the opportunity, for which I felt very privileged, to sit down with historical documents. If I had been given a large group of diaries from the Civil War, I would have tackled it with the same vigor, and it would have meant as much to me. I would not have chosen to debate whether the generals in the Civil War truly believed in the causes they were fighting for. I would be a historian simply editing it."

Project Blue Book today seems so tame and old hat—a UFO sighting here, a sighting there—with nothing about crop circles, or abductions, or Men in Black.

"Well, I suppose, if you're familiar with the 'Project Blue Book' material, but, of course, there are people coming onto this subject new every year, and they're picking it up and using it as a resource and reference material. There's nothing about Men in Black, or crop circles, because that wasn't happening then. Abductions were going on, but only a select group such as Timothy Beckley, John Keel and myself were being excited about it. No one in the standard research area, or rather the orthodox standard research area, was paying any attention to that. Now, of course, it's de rigueur, but at that time, we were the weirdos concerned about such matters."

Revelation: The Divine Fire (Prentice-Hall, 1973) was Steiger's first major book, and introduced the concept of channeling as a major element of the New Age movement. In it, he writes, "The gift of Spirit did not cease with the prophets and saints of antiquity—it is a vital, continuing process which observes no denominational boundaries."

In this book, Steiger makes numerous mentions of his own encounters with spiritual beings. The inspiration for the book itself came after a visitation from a hooded spiritual being. He also tells of seeing an elfin entity at the kitchen window of his parents' farmhouse as a kid, an episode of which he writes, "If not a real encounter, then the single most vivid dream of my childhood." Mr. Steiger, are you an abductee?

"Not at all. Not that I remember, anyway."

Throughout your books, you write that these aliens insist they do not have the right to interfere with man's free will. What about these alien abductions being reported?

"If abductions exist in a physical reality, then from the aliens' aspect, they may or may not be thinking they are interfering. I'll use an analogy: Let's say some scientists are in a remote village in the Amazon, doing some research there. But they're alien to these villagers, and the villagers regard them with suspicion. But the scientists have deduced that cholera or some epidemic is about to break out, so they contact the local authorities, and all these doctors arrive in helicopters, descending from the sky, rounding everybody up, giving them shots then off they go again.

"Now the village wise men have to determine: Who were these beings? The villagers had pain where the shots were given, and some died anyway because they got the shots too late. And others were saved but they don't even know it. You can see how all that could lead to an entire mystique. Now what these villagers don't realize, perhaps even the wisest of them, is that their entire village was being saved. And that may be a part of what's happening with our abductions, in a way we don't understand."

What do you suspect these aliens are going to do with all this data that they're collecting?

"Maybe we are being tested and poked and probed because of AIDS or some other epidemic, and then the resulting data will come through a dream or a vision to some research scientist who will be 'inspired' to find the correct chemical combinations that will heal people. Now that is theoretical, but all of this is theoretical."

In his book *Gods Of Aquarius* (Harcourt Brace Jovanovich, 1976), Steiger interviewed a couple of New Age prophets who were calling themselves Bo and Peep. Their cult was known as Human Individual Metamorphosis (HIM), and even back then, Marshall Applewhite (Bo) was preaching a physical transportation to Heaven via a UFO. Twenty of their followers had already disappeared, seemingly right off the face of the Earth, never to be heard from again.

In the 1990s, Peep was dead, and Applewhite was now calling himself Do, and was leader of the Heaven's Gate

Marshall Applewhite
Leader of Heaven's Gate Cult
(Courtesy of Signet Books)

cult. Thirty-eight members followed Do in suicide, hoping to link up with a UFO supposedly following in the wake of the Comet Hale-Bopp.

Mr. Steiger, what are your observations on the cult phenomenon as we near the coming New Age?

> "Many UFO contactees that I have interviewed over the past thirty years have felt a great urgency to relay messages that they are convinced were given them by extraterrestrial beings. Nearly all of them sense a time of coming Earth changes, a time of fire and destruction. But whereas traditional or fundamental Christian prophets see this period of cleansing as the End Time, most of the UFO contactees see this period as one of transition between ages rather than a Day of Judgement."

Mother Mary Speaks To Us (Dutton Books, 1996), co-written by Steiger with his wife Sherry, is a study of the worldwide appearances of the Blessed Virgin, the Queen of Heaven. The book chronicles the increasing number of manifestations of the Great Mother image since the 1960s. These rapturous encounters have been taking place in homes, in churches, and in open fields, often leaving behind a flurry of miraculous healings in her wake.

It appears to be the Age of Mother Mary. She has announced that her appearances have to do with the imminent Second Coming, and she urges all people to have faith in God. Her statues have also been known to cry tears or blood—"The Weeping Madonna"—foretelling of a terrible ordeal if people do not return to God.

Again, I'm prompted to wonder: Why would she give her message to a select few, usually peasant children, often telling them secrets that they're not supposed to reveal? Still, I found *Mother Mary Speaks To Us* to be a very thought-provoking book, and I find great hope in the possibility that a Great

Mother image is out there somewhere watching over us.

> "I'm glad that you enjoyed that book. Many
> people have been very generous in their
> praise and comments. Certainly, I admit I
> can't answer a lot of questions. I ask more
> questions than I answer actually. But I like to
> think, I like to theorize. But we are definitely
> in the age of the Mother."

Around the world, these visionaries of Mother Mary are telling us that she is also forewarning us about UFOs, i.e.—"Be not afeared, for you are being allowed to see what Satan plans to delude Mankind with. They are agents of Hell in transport. Recognize them; they are not a figment of man's imagination. They are present in your atmosphere, and they will become more dominant as the fight goes on for souls. Make it known. Satan seeks to confuse you."—Veronica (1973).

"There is life on many planets who also worship the Creator of all. Some of these beings are known to visit Earth. But where there is contentment, there is no fear. Where there is no fear, one truly knows how to live in the flow of life."—Watson (1995).

"There will be an increased number of UFO sightings, and with the new renaissance for humankind there will also appear a new species of humanity upon Earth. Prayers can alleviate and do not delude yourselves into thinking that you are helpless."—Kirkwood (1995).

Sounds ominous to me, Mr. Steiger. We are in "fellowship" with these aliens, right? UFOs: good or evil?

> "No one can answer that. We live in a world
> of dualism and so we immediately assume
> they are dualistic. But I think that if they are
> physical beings, then just as we are physical
> beings and we have some rotten apples in
> our barrels, and some saints walking among
> us at the same time, I would assume that
> these entities do, too. Just because they are
> technologically superior does not make

them morally superior. On the other hand,
they may be regarding us as Class 101 in
Biology, simply observing, or as I said before,
saving our butts, and we don't even realize
it."

As I sat listening to Steiger's vocal qualities on the cassette,
what I heard was a man exhibiting extreme patience, both in
answering my questions, and in pursuing life's boundless mysteries. So Steiger is pursuing patience, and since patience is a
virtue, he must be a virtuous man. And why not? Anyone who
gets to spend a career delving into spiritual realms must be riding on grace. Even if they do encounter that more-questions-
than-answers phenomenon.

Throughout Steiger's books, I read only uplifting words,
and as a believer in the power of positive thinking I can appre-
ciate that. Then the cassette came to an end, and I suddenly
recalled that I forgot to ask Steiger one all-important question:

Mr. Steiger, you write that these channelers say that the
Elohim cannot return en masse until the inhabitants of Earth
display a greater ability to live together in fraternity and love.
Since we both know that this is unlikely to happen—are we
facing the ghastly specter of nuclear annihilation?

(I can already hear him reply that our destiny probably lies
in our own hands.)

And if we are unable to save ourselves, will these spiritual
multidimensional beings come down in time to save us? And if
they do truly want to help humankind, what are they waiting
for? Armageddon? So as to make an impression?

Feel free to answer any of these questions, Mr. Steiger.
Obviously, they all lead to that ultimate question of identity:
Who are we? Or rather, who are we to be worth a damn for
these beings to care?

Even the Man of Aquarius might admit that he can't answer
that one, but I bring it up in hope that he'll do some research
on the subject then write a book about it, to let us all know.

The Fellowship: Spiritual Contact Between Humans and Outer Space Beings
(Ivy Books, 1988)
        Brad Steiger

For a complimentary copy of the "Steiger Questionnaire of Mystical, Paranormal, and UFO Experiences," write to:
        Timewalker Productions
        P.O. Box 434
        Forest City, Iowa 50436

Chapter Six

The Voice
of Dreamland

Imagine the quiet stillness

of the early morning hours

When only the stars seem to

trouble a black sky

and the voice carries...

Now add late night talk radio

where the most popular topic

is the paranormal

The Voice
of Dreamland

"From coast to coast and around the world via the Internet..."

Imagine that you have a nationally-syndicated radio talk show discussing the paranormal, and between your on-the-air guests and your call-in listeners, you and your audience are kept abreast of the UFO situation.

"Good morning or good evening, depending on your time zone..."

And throughout these late night hours, you guide your show through topics like outer space and things like dreams over which we have no control.

"This is Art Bell from the High Desert..."

What if you thought you saw something ominous coming? Would you share it with your listeners?

"First time caller—you're on the line..."

Art Bell is the Voice of Dreamland. His rich voice sounds earnest and enthusiastic over the airwaves, even though he receives few true answers. Few proofs, anyway. On his World Wide Web page, however, he'll show all worthwhile photos and allow you to make your own judgments.

"Wild Card Line. Hello, you're on the air..."

Commercial pilots contact Bell to recount to him their

incredible UFO engagements, but fear to reveal themselves because the country is still too negative. Military men confide in Bell as to just how correct the ET trail is that he is pursuing, but they cannot come forth in fear of losing their pensions. The Government is still too frightened.

Yet despite the lack of hard evidence, Bell's been observing the signs long enough to believe "Things are coming to some sort of crescendo. It may result in Earth changes but either way, it's gonna scare the pants off people."

THE QUICKENING

Today's Trends, Tomorrow's World

ART BELL

(Courtesy of Paper Chase Press)

And so after being on the air for over thirty years pursuing the paranormal boundaries in all directions, and with a listening audience around the world keeping him updated with the latest changes, Bell believes he knows what is happening. He wrote a book about it. He called it *The Quickening*.

If you want a happy read, keep away from this book. With chapter titles such as "Technology" and "Government," Bell's obviously well-read and in touch with the changes going on in the world around us. And he insists that we're all gradually waking up to the same thing. "Nearly every aspect of life in every part of our world," he writes, "is accelerating, changing, quickening. I coined the term 'the Quickening' to describe the overall movement."

Take, for instance, our technology, which, in the blink of an eye, is outdated. And since technology is essentially the driving force behind the Quickening, this area of our lives is gaining in leaps and bounds. Bell lists two of the most notable technologies as being: (a) Rockets: "A nuclear bomb is the most ominous technology in existence today. Ironic, isn't it? The technology created to protect us now dangles over our heads" and (b) Computers: "We now truly live in an information age, and nowhere is the computer's role in the Quickening more obvious than on the Internet. No one imagined the Internet would become what it is today."

By the year 2001, it is estimated that there will be 100 million web sites on the Internet, with over one billion users daily, making this planet a truly global village. TV is slowly waving good-bye as the Internet screen gradually becomes our own personalized information and entertainment center.

Our uncertain future can also be seen in our planet's struggling ecosystem. Life is vanishing off our planet at an alarming rate. We're facing a widening gap in the ozone layer, a thickening pollution in our water and atmosphere, and increasingly violent and radically-changing weather patterns.

According to NASA, eight of the ten warmest years in recorded history were in the 1990s, with 1998 ranking as the hottest year on record. Antarctic glaciers are rapidly melting, and forecasters predict that it won't be long before a rise in ocean levels and the resulting weather change should be noticeable to the average person on the street.

"But no matter how you turn it," writes Bell, "the number one problem when it to comes the environment around us— the air, the water, the soil—is people. Whatever angles environmental groups decide to approach the destruction of the Earth from, it still comes down to a basic fact: Our society is a pack of consumers."

Bell believes that America has become literally a "throw-away society," and, of course, the irony here is that while the rest of the world is starving, America is besieged by an epidemic of obesity. He writes: "Our society is catering more and more to self, to narcissism. Our priorities have been derailed. Maybe we think we will never pay a price for such thinking but that is not reality. As a result, the very foundations of our society shift under our feet like sand on a troubled shore."

And he points the finger at the U.S. Government as being

part of the problem and not the solution. What they argue about in Washington has less and less relevance to the daily lives of the American people.

"Flag? What flag?" Bell asks. "Patriotism is not taken very seriously any more. Saluting the flag and singing the national anthem are no longer done out of pride. I remember a time where you had respect for the President, when agencies like the CIA or FBI were something to respect. But those days are over."

And perhaps the saddest changes in our Quickening society are those reflected in our children. A young generation is growing up without the "traditional" family—a mother and a father and the child living together under the same roof. Meanwhile, the children must cope with problems such as increased drug use, rising violence, and rampant pornography. Statistics for rape and murder among the young is rising dramatically.

Bell writes: "What kind of world do we live in when a child has absolutely no hope for the future? What kind of a world will be built by people who cannot construct stable relationships and family lives? In all our brilliance humans are able to devise the most fantastic machines and gadgets, and yet we are unable to control the way we behave in this world."

It's for all of these reasons that Bell feels we're headed toward a one Global Government, built upon a global economy. This one governing body is coming to control all economic and political activity worldwide, but he also believes this will be a good thing: "To achieve prosperity, peace, and a clean environment will require a collective effort on the part of the entire world, a common effort playing by the same rules."

What could actually trigger this Global Government? It could be anything from a financial crisis to increased terrorism, or even alien visitors who finally reveal themselves openly. Whatever it is, Bell suggests that it is just around the corner.

He also notes that in these quick-moving times, there has been a distinct move away from traditional religion. He's seen a surge in the exploration of the spirit through what is called the

New Age movement, the belief that "All is One" and that a common energy flows through all things. This power of Creation—God—exists in all things, and therefore humans are divine.

Bell describes it as the most rapidly-growing form of spirituality in the world today. And we could certainly use a dose of Spirit-mindedness in these times, especially when you consider what Bell describes as "a cruel twist in our Quickening world": nuclear proliferation. "If just one nuclear bomb goes off, we instantly have a type of pollution that we can't deal with. And once it gets started, it just keeps on killing and killing."

Few will disagree that the planet today is in nuclear peril, and despite the fact that almost five hundred nuclear reactors are operating worldwide, no one knows how to properly dispose of nuclear waste. Meanwhile, terrorist factions armed with nuclear weapons have been cited as the "most immediate threat to free-world security."

Bell throws into this bubbling cauldron increasing plagues: "Cholera, malaria, tuberculosis and, yes, the bubonic plague, are all coming back, carving inroads into our smug confidence in survival."

He also mixes into this ominous brew the potential of biological warfare: "Biological agents are considered to be one of the least costly and most effective means of destroying an enemy. Some have called biological warheads 'the poor man's nuclear bomb.'"

And keep in mind our ever-increasing human population. It took man from the dawn of civilization to 1830 to reach a population of one billion. By 1990, we had reached six billion. The world population is now doubling every forty years, with the human race expanding by a 225,000 births per day. It's another fearsome reminder that we're not in control, and basically it all adds up to the Quickening.

And as if we don't have enough to be concerned with, we are now having alien visitations. UFO reports throughout the world have skyrocketed in the past five decades, everything from encounters to abductions.

Bell writes: "The one common experience shared by these abductees is the impression that these aliens wield incredible powers, and nearly all of them felt it was a strong spiritual experience. Will these aliens make themselves conspicuous, and if they do, what will happen? Mass panic or calm acceptance? It is anyone's guess where all this is leading."

And that is the broad premise of Bell's book, as well as his late night talk show known as *Coast to Coast AM* (weeknights), or *Dreamland* (weekends).

Bell broadcasts out of his own home in the desert of

Art Bell's studio—"broadcasting to ten million listeners, isolated from us all." (Courtesy of Paper Chase Press)

Pahrump, Nevada ("living in the middle of nowhere massages my soul"), not far from a controversial zone called Area 51, often referred to as "Dreamland" for the strange aircraft test flights said to occur there. Many UFOlogists believe this is where the U.S. Government houses spacecraft from out of this world.

The topics of Bell's talk show run the paranormal gamut from A to Z. An example would include—

The (Ret.) Col. Corso show and a look at the Roswell Crash, where a spacecraft supposedly crashed in the desert and alien bodies were found. Corso gave us the military's point of view. According to the Colonel, human body parts were also found on the crashed spaceship. President Truman was reportedly very upset. The U.S. Government suddenly discovers that the aliens had lied to them at previous meetings, they had killed some of our servicemen, and when you take into consideration that all UFO abductees are fearful of these "beings," the military has to consider them unfriendly.

Whitley Strieber, another guest on his show (the author of *Communion* and a UFO abductee himself), confirms this suspicion. He found these aliens to be "very negative—very scary—not at all our friends. Remember, these are visitors and some of them are very tough birds."

There was the caller who informed Bell that he shot a Bigfoot, and he was willing to lead Bell to the gravesite where he buried it, but Bell's callers reminded him that if the beast is part human, the man could be tried for murder. So the man backed out.

Then there was the lady caller who said that since getting hit on the head, she's had four premonitions, all which came true, and now she's had a fifth one that she wants to share. She said that when a UFO lands, and it will be soon, the person stepping from that spacecraft will look exactly like John F. Kennedy.

Bell: "You're going to say it's the Antichrist."

She was taken aback. "How did you know?"

Bell: "You're not the first to have that premonition."

The prophecy concerning the Antichrist is that a charismatic figure will receive a head wound and die, then later be revived from the seeming dead.

There was that classic night that Bell talked to Mel, owner of Mel's Hole (Oregon), which is so far a bottomless pit. People are throwing garbage down that hole by the ton. No sound—no echo—nothing. So Mel finally drops a weighted fishing line down into the hole, and begins measuring the output. He's thus far at an incredible 80,000 feet—sixteen miles! (The deepest trench in the world is the Marianas Trench at seven miles, about 37,000 feet, below sea level.)

Bell suggested that someone be lowered down into the hole on a rope. A media person, perhaps. A young man then called in and said that he would volunteer to go down into the hole, on two conditions.

Bell: "What conditions?"

Volunteer: "First I want a cage—in the event something at the bottom tries to eat me."

Bell:"So they can pull you up when they hear you scream?"

Volunteer:"That's my second condition. I'd want an instant 'up' button."

Bell still insisted they send down a media person.

I especially liked the caller who insisted that the intelligentsia had lied about Pi. Instead of its ratio of 3.1415 extending into a series of non-repeating decimals, the real Pi is a series of repeating decimals. The conspiracy is that 'those in the know' know and use the correct Pi, and that's how they keep their control over us.

Bell (exasperated):"They lied about Pi?"

And, of course, there is that ever-fascinating phenomenon known as crop circles. "We are having the most remarkable 'crop' season," Bell states on air. "It's incredible, and you can take a look at the latest formations on my web site. They are so intricate, so perfect, so beautiful, that I refused to believe that a human being has done them. And this season's crop circles will absolutely take your breath away."

Bell believes that the atomic detonation was a key moment for ETs to start actively getting involved in a very close monitoring of planet Earth. Cattle mutilations and crop circles are part of this monitoring. "It makes you wonder," he asks, "if we got involved in a nuclear war, would they step in?"

A later guest supplied us with what he thought to be the key to deciphering crop circles: Trace the crop circle on a sheet of paper, put a hole in the middle, and spin it on a pencil. In the spinning, they take on a 3-D effect, and you can read the "hieroglyphics."

One night, Bell opened up the "Time Line," for those travelers who are here from another time. In other words, time travelers. And don't call unless you're a time traveler, the honest-to-goodness real thing.

Every time traveler who called in started off by saying that they were not allowed to say certain things or to answer certain questions. It has to do with "The Butterfly Effect," proposing the notion that a butterfly stirring the air in Hong Kong can produce a storm system in L.A. One thing leads to another. In other words, any wrong thing they say could affect the future and might be used against them.

At its simplest, these visitors described time travel as having something to do with shifting of the temporal lobes in the brain. And they were all in agreement that they saw alien contact imminent. They also said that we are having an increase in crop circles, which is a form of communication between alien species, because we are having more visitors because these are interesting times.

And then there was that month in July when a man named Richard Hoagland hogged the spotlight and told us:

(1) when the Mars Probe and its landrover Sojourner arrived at Mars, we would lose all radio contact with them, and it was during this blackout that NASA would set about doing its dirty work—photographing the Cydonia region and the Face on Mars, and

(2) all of this coincided with an astrological conjunction that had the Sphinx in Egypt staring directly up at the Face on Mars, and this was somehow linked to a symbolical rising in Phoenix, Arizona, where a massive UFO sighting had just taken place. All this was building up to the UFOs making a second, more impressive, appearance, this time to the mass media!

Meanwhile, Army troops were supposedly being sent into the outlying areas, FBI were flooding into the city, and martial law was just around the corner. The Government was going to try and suppress this second mass sighting, astrologically predicted to happen between July 20-22. A city councilwoman was also being harassed for admitting to having seen the UFO and seeking some answers.

So I went and told all my family and friends: UFOs will be revealing themselves to us by July 22nd! My brother and I bet a box of Cheez-its on it.

The date came and went. There were no shenanigans with the landrover on Mars, no massive UFO revelations over Phoenix. And it wasn't so much the cost of the box of crackers that I regretted losing, but that once again, the rumors turned out to be just that—more wild hair-raising rumors. As Bell

Author and his brother Tom

would say, "We're getting some pretty downwind information here." Plus I guess the FBI and Army troops had all wasted their time. I went out and bought my brother a box of Cheez-its, and Hoagland laid low from Bell's radio show for a while.

(Hoagland's *The Monuments of Mars* was the first video to point to those provocative photos taken of the Face on Mars by NASA's Viking 1 probe in 1976. NASA, however, doesn't appear too interested in researching the structures, preferring instead to gather rocks.)

And why, asked a caller, were we fooling around with a remote-controlled landrover on Mars? Why weren't we using miniature helicopters?

Bell: "No atmosphere?"

"Then what about the fact that the module came down with a parachute? There was enough atmosphere for that."

Good point.

I'm tempted to call Bell "Mr. Time Compression," if only as a badge of honor for some of the nonsense that he's had to endure. Like the time a Pentagon official came out to explain away the Roswell incident by showing us some film footage of a weather balloon experiment and crash test dummies. The Colonel stated that this filmed experiment would account for the Roswell crash and the bodies supposedly found.

Unfortunately for the Colonel, some knowledgeable person in the audience questioned him about the fact that the film was taken in 1953, which did little to explain a crash in 1947. This Pentagon official then boldly told the reporter that he was remembering it wrong, and this was due to time compression. The Colonel squeezed his fist into his palm as a visual.

Immediately after that, Bell started explaining away all "unexplainables" by using the phrase, "Well, it must have been time compression." Some believe that the Pentagon purposely sent this Colonel out to fan the flames, by using phrases such as "this puts a whole new spin on it."Talk about a Freudian slip. (Perhaps this was a subliminal way of urging UFO enthusiasts to continue their investigations.)

Bell has seen a UFO, but he can't say what it was. As I said, proofs are hard to come by. Opinions and speculations, however, are why his listeners tune in, and that's all part of the craziness that makes for a great late night talk show.

Bell takes all calls live and unscreened, and as a result the discussions can range from conspiracies (things are usually hidden out in the open), to reverse speech (where people tell the truth backwards), to the possibility that the words written on the Pope's miter add up to 666.

"And what you see on the surface is just an inkling of what's going on," says Bell. "We can connect the dots. I don't, however, like where the dots obviously lead."

Bell agreed to an interview through his editor, who then faxed me his answers. He gets mail by the bin full; he receives thousands of E-mail messages daily; he reads hundreds of faxes day and night. Bell taking time in between all that to answer this author's questions is appreciated.

In *The Quickening*, Mr. Bell, you write that Mother Earth is getting ready to get our attention. There's going to be a big change, and it's

Art Bell
(Courtesy of Barbara Weaver)

not very far off because of the Quickening upon us. Should people be headed for caves?

"There has definitely been a distinct acceleration of nearly everything in life," replied Bell. "We are all affected by what is going on and unfortunately, much of it does appear to be destructive. Our society seems to be unraveling as the family disintegrates with a continued high divorce rate and what appears to be an increasing disregard for our fellow man. Global economic and political powers appear to be positioning for what will most likely be world control by one governing body at some point, perhaps both liberating and limiting our personal autonomy as free citizens.

"Should we be headed for caves? Well, no matter what I said, I think people have their own minds and would make their own decisions. I have been called paranoid and a doomsayer, but I think that it is natural for people to react to the truth in this way, especially if it is not the most pleasant reality. Other people embrace these concepts willingly and might even incorporate them into their daily life."

What is an alternative to heading for caves?

"In terms of what we can do as an alternative, that calls for overall change as a society. Yes, there are some things we probably cannot undo (i.e., the increasingly corrupted ecosystem), but we can change the way we treat other people. This is very important, and something we can all do. The world of tomorrow is destined to be a much different one than the one we live in today, and we have to prepare ourselves mentally for that."

You wrote that the downside of the Internet is that it will enable people to avoid physical contact with the outside world. Ironic, isn't it, that there you sit alone in a room, speaking to ten million listeners, but isolated from us all.

"Ironic is the right word for it. The technology that we depend upon so heavily today, that in fact we take for granted in many ways, has a double-edged sword effect upon us. On the one hand, technology does isolate us, as you say. On the other, because it blankets everything we do, it draws us together in a global sense. In terms of what I do, I couldn't do my job without it."

Tell us what it's like to be alone in your studio, hosting a show that sends your voice all over the world.

"Mostly, when I'm doing my show, I try not to think how many millions of people might be listening. If I think about that, I sweat! I just concentrate on what I know, what I have prepared for, and I relish the knowledge that people everywhere are getting exposed to and have a forum to discuss things they are interested in.

"*Coast to Coast* and my other show *Dreamland* have changed my life. I have a good sense of what is going on out there. I feel I have my finger on the metaphorical 'pulse' of the people. It's been a real education. And I try to stay open-minded about everything. You just never know what will come up next, or what you can learn. And that is one of the most marvelous things (and sometimes scary) about broadcasting the way I do."

In your first book, *The Art Of Talk*, you wrote: "As a radio talk show host, I am in the unique position of influencing people." You are truly a nationwide star. Do you feel any moral obligation because your voice is heard by literally millions of people?

> "Moral obligation...well, there are times that a subject will come up or an event will happen and people will try and point fingers at me for it, like with Heaven's Gate. I still maintain that no matter who I have on my show or what I talk about, my listeners are able to discern for themselves and make their own decisions about what they believe and what they think is b.s. So in terms of moral obligation, I am a talk show host and I present things that ordinarily are not presented on a large media scale. Do I feel bad if something terrible happens? Of course. Do I assume responsibility for it? Not usually."

For all of your listeners out there who would like to get to know a little something about Art Bell: You were born in 1945, you love your wife like a soulmate, and your two passions are radio and flying. You've also participated in two world record-breaking stunts: (1) the longest continuous broadcast (115 hours and 15 minutes) which you call a stupid stunt that might have done you some permanent physical and mental damage, and (2) the longest continuous see-saw record (57 hours) which took place during a time when you describe yourself as "young and stupid." What's next?

> "I did those things when I was much, much younger. I mean, I was pretty crazy and reckless back then. So if you're asking, would I do that stuff again? Well, I did parasailing. That's pretty close, I did that a few years ago. That was great. I love that feeling of flying through the air. But endurance stuff, well, I'm sure I'm stubborn enough, but I'm not sure I'm that reckless at this point."

And are you happy with your status, both on the radio and in life?

"Professionally, I am doing exactly what I want to be doing at the level I want to be doing it. Personally, I would like to fly. Nothing fancy, like a fighter jet, but if I could become a private pilot and fly a Cessna or a propjet at some point. My biggest fantasy is about flying. When I was little, I rode down a hill in my red wagon or jumped out of a barn loft door to experience the sensation of being in the air.

"In terms of my life, I want to keep traveling, seeing and learning about new things and places. I want to find out the answers to two major questions: 1) Is there a conscious existence or life beyond the one we now know? And 2) Are we being visited by beings from this world or another? These are the questions I wonder about, and I know these are the questions the people of the world wonder about. And the second one may be answered in our lifetimes. So I am exploring that more than jumping off the sides of barns anymore."

You wrote of "America's Heavy Load" where you suggest that it will be the debt of this country, both on an individual and national level, that will ultimately cause our collapse. You say your prayers are for the return of earlier values, the glue that made America a great country in the first place.

"Society and people's behavior reflects that the innocence that America had back in the 1950s has been long lost. Many of us have a hard time seeing that everything around us is not okay. People are starving in countries far away from us, but women are also being raped and murdered in the house next door. We complacently watch violence on television and in movies, but want our children to be protected from such horrors as drugs, alcohol and sex at young age.

Where should society start to clean up its act?

"Society and societal ills have progressed at such a rapid rate and along such negative trends that most of the issues that need to be addressed are out of human control. I think that instead of a practice of common decency, our priorities have been derailed and our values have been buried in a sea of selfishness. And most issues have to be addressed, when they can, at an individual level."

And to whom do you pray for a return of these earlier values?

"I do believe in a Creator. When I have a conversation with a preacher or a priest, or a minister, even those people who come in suits on bicycles and knock on the door, I generally drive them crazy. Still, I enjoy talking to them all. I ask them questions that inevitably lead them to say, 'But you must have faith.' And I simply explain that I cannot have faith. I must have proof to have faith. I must see something that is tangible to me. This, of course, just drives them all up a tree. I love doing it.

"In terms of spirituality and praying, I have recently become much more spiritual in very nontraditional ways. I didn't suddenly run down to church and I am still not doing that. I'm definitely a reincarnationist and I believe that what we do in this life affects everything—now and afterwards.

What is the most unusual or favorite story that you've come across in your years of broadcasting?

"Oh geez, there are so many. Let's see, I

thought the whole Hale-Bopp story was pretty strange. Heaven's Gate was spooky. Especially since they were trying to blame me. One time a guy had me pretty well believing that there was a huge earthquake about to happen; he had all this documentation and it looked very real. That was a scary one. I look for and enjoy the most when I can find a story that has no definite answer, something controversial that will stimulate interesting discussion. After all, that's what I do. I'm in the business of controversy, human nature and the outer edge."

A couple of nights later, I was listening to *Dreamland* on the radio, and Bell was interviewing the ex-cohost of the Pat Robertson Show. Rev. Robertson is a TV evangelist who preached something to the effect that "we should stone all UFO believers because they are idolaters," and then quoted something in Deuteronomy to back up his statement. So in defense of Robertson's statement, this ex-cohost says: "But if you look back at the Old Testament, God did many bloody things."

I wanted to tell her "Wrong, ma'am, God did no bloody thing. Mankind did every bloody thing," but I could not get through on the phone lines. Even though Bell has five lines, you have to have the luck of the Irish or his private number to get through.

And then I realized how lucky I was to capture an interview with this man who has an ear to the world. And a voice to deliver it back out again. And one thing I will say for Bell is that as a talk show host, he never sounds self-righteous. He comes across as intelligent and firm about what he knows, but gives all callers equal footing. He says a good talk show host lets his guests tell their story and doesn't interrupt. I know it makes for a good talk show.

So there in the quiet of the night, listening to Bell's rich voice coming in over the speakers, it felt like it was just him and me, listening to all the crazies out there, and half-identifying with many of them. The occasional static coming in over the speakers, fading the words in and out, only added to the thoughtfulness of the late hour.

And if I could have Bell's attention once more, I have a hypothetical question I'd like to ask him, but most likely his reply would be the same as he wrote in his book—"The answer lies in the mirror that we all look into daily."

Other than that, each of us must conclude for ourselves how to best come to terms with the Quickening.

P.S. They lied about Pi?

*The Quickening: Today's Trends,
Tomorrow's World* (1997)
    Art Bell

The Art Of Talk (1995)
    Art Bell

Both books are available from:
    Paper Chase Press
    8175 South Virginia Street, #850-D
    Reno, Nevada 89511

For information on *Coast To Coast AM*
and *Dreamland*, check your local radio
listings, or www.artbell.com

Chapter Seven

The Eye
On The Sky

What if we told you

   what the Government doesn't

   want you to know – is on video?

And if you saw the unbelievable

   could you believe

   your eyes and ears?

Still – it's only what the ETs

   want you to see

The Eye
On The Sky

Videotape. The bane of our existence? Or the Great Enlightener? Can we really believe only half of what we see? Or any of what we hear?

The time lapse between the actual recording and release into the hands of the public can be considerable, often passing through many filters and many hands. But as you sit watching these UFO videos—you sit transfixed. Whys and wherefores immediately rise to mind as common sense is pushed aside. What else can you do when presented with supernatural images of disappearing spacecraft...magically-complex crop circles...constructed ruins on Mars? And despite your pressing doubts, or perhaps because of them, you want to view these videos again, if only to see if you can detect some flaw.

And if you do find a blemish, does it mean you can dismiss the whole UFO phenomenon, or just that series of frames?

When I first spoke to Tim Crawford on the phone, I found him to be open and enthusiastic to the idea of being interviewed. He's well-versed in the UFO intrigue. As Founder and President of "UFO Central," he claims to have seen every one of his company's over 1200 videos. When it comes down to the paranormal captured on tape, I'd heard that Crawford was the

Tim Crawford

man to see.

When I first met him in his office, his phones were ringing off the hook. Crawford, tall, thin, and bearded, seemed to be answering five phones at once. He gave me a high-five sign, then one by one put all lines on hold to tell me that he had a Top Five Video list—videos that go far beyond what we see on broadcast TV. He promised me astonishing, mind-boggling possibilities. He had me hooked. I went home with the Top Five.

The #1 video on the list was Bob Lazar's *Excerpts From The Government Bible* (1991–50 min.). I first heard of Lazar when he gave a bold but brief interview on a TV talk show, disguised as a silhouette. He was in hiding at the time, living out of a P.O. Box. He finally made this tape and went public because his life had been threatened and he felt he had nothing to lose. By doing so, he became the first person with any credibility to break the silence of Area 51 by introducing us to physical evidence of aliens.

Physical evidence?

As a nuclear physicist, Lazar deals with the Periodic Table. This is a chart listing all of the chemical elements that make up the physical world according to their atomic number, starting with 1-H (hydrogen), the simplest molecule, to 112-Uub (ununbiium), which is radioactive. Only the first 94 of these elements, up to and including plutonium, appear naturally on earth; the rest were artificially created in laboratories.

Lazar claims to have been employed as a civilian physicist by the U.S. Navy at a site known as S4 in Area 51 during 1988. It was his job to "reverse-engineer" the propulsion system of an alien vehicle. Reverse-engineering is the art of taking apart a finished product in order to find out what makes it work. The goal was to see if the propulsion system could be duplicated with Earth materials.

Before Lazar could get much accomplished, however, he was fired (dismissed for being unstable, due to a divorce looming

*Bob Lazar
(Courtesy of Bob Lazar)*

in his future), but not before he saw how the spacecraft operated. His conclusion: The craft operated on Element 115, which is what makes interstellar flight a possibility. Since there are only 112 elements on our atomic chart, Element 115 is not yet known to this Earth.

Still, since physical matter (i.e. a spacecraft) cannot travel faster than the speed of light (186,000 miles per second, 669 million mph), interstellar travel is a physical impossibility.

According to Lazar, the alien mode of interstellar travel has nothing to do traveling in a line near the speed of light. As he explains on the tape, "When you're dealing with space/time, the fastest way from point A to B is not a straight line, but to distort or bend the space/time between them, bringing point A and B closer together. Thus you have traveled a great distance with little linear movement, in little or no time." In other words, by folding space, they can travel anywhere in the Universe without moving.

It's a scientific given that gravity can distort space and time and light, but how does one generate a gravitational field strong enough to distort their own space and time?

According to Lazar, the answer is Element 115, which he claims radiates "anti-matter," an exact counterpart of matter, with a charge and a spin that is the opposite of all matter. Not found on Earth but apparently possessed by these visiting aliens, this element is what allows them to generate their own gravity field and travel these vast distances through time and space.

Lazar claims to have been inside one of the flying saucers, where he worked on its reactor. He states that the center level housed the control consoles and seats, both of which were too small and too low to the floor to be functional for an adult human.

On tape, he tells us: "I was never allowed on the upper level of the disc, so I can't enlighten you as to what the porthole areas are, although I can assure you they were not portholes." He also alleges to have witnessed one of the saucers fully functional and in flight, but no, he unfortunately didn't get to go for a ride.

The second part of Lazar's tape was even more fascinating. Lazar claims that as part of his indoctrination into the S4 program, he was allowed brief readings out of some blue folders which gave him an overview of the alien situation. The pages explained how the technology that he was working on had been brought to Earth by visitors from the Zeta Reticuli star system. Today we know them as Greys.

Groom Lake (Area 51)
Lat N37, 14.66
Lon W115 47.61
(Courtesy of U.S. Geological Survey)

The pages in the blue folders told how the U.S. Government had been exchanging information and hardware with the "beings" at that S4 site for years until a violent conflict brought the program to an abrupt halt. UFO folklore says the confrontation ended in a complete victory for the aliens, leaving more than two dozen U.S. military officers dead in its wake.

When the "beings" departed, the military began a reverse-engineering program on the saucers left behind. They removed the propulsion device from one, and when they cut the reactor open, the resulting explosion killed two of the engineers. Lazar had been hired to replace one of those men.

The blue folders told how the "beings" said that man was the product of externally-corrected evolution, and that humankind as a species had been genetically altered sixty-five times. The pages always referred to human beings as "containers," without saying what we were containers of.

For Lazar, the bottom line is "It's the right of every person on Earth to know that there is physical evidence which proves that there is life elsewhere, and that at least one form of that life has been here." That evidence is apparently hidden away at the S4 Sector in Area 51 of the "Dreamland" complex.

The tape ended all too soon for my liking, at a scant hour. There were no eye-popping stunts, but if you took notes, it all seemed to work out on paper. But why didn't he go into what he thought those "portholes" were?

(Lazar did add in a later book, *UFOs And The Alien Presence: Six Viewpoints* [2020 Group, 1991], that he also saw photographs of aliens, but they were more or less autopsy reports.)

The second video on the list was *UFOs: Above And Beyond* (1997–50 min). Hosted by James Doohan, *Star Trek's* "Scotty," this video was a compelling feast of seldom-seen UFO footage.

Since the space race first began between the USA and the USSR, NASA logs show that practically all of their Gemini and Apollo missions encountered UFOs. One of their early code words for UFOs was "Santa Claus," but it wasn't long before outside listeners caught on, and soon after that, NASA began scrambling their radio transmissions. Perhaps our most impressive UFO sightings are those with deep space as a background.

Note the strange white glow hovering over Apollo 12 astronaut (Courtesy of NASA)

Taken by the Apollo 13 mission, an unknown object glows near the moon's surface (Courtesy of NASA)

Deep Space, 1969: The day before their historic landing on the moon, the Apollo 11 crew filmed some luminous discs in casual orbit around the moon. Another series of frames taken by the later Apollo 12 mission shows a bright object flying over the moon's surface at tremendous speed.

Deep Space, 1976: NASA's Viking probe, taking pictures of the surface of Mars, begins relaying back a series of photos showing unnatural structures, including a "face" carved out of a large mesa. NASA's official explanation for the anomaly was that the complete picture contained missing data as the Viking's cameras malfunctioned and could not transmit the remaining information.

Washington, D.C., 1952: Still photos show the nation's capital being buzzed by a squadron of saucer-shaped lights, flying in formation for eyewitnesses to snap pictures. It's been estimated that the "lights" were traveling an estimated 7000 mph. The Air Force said that it was a "temperature inversion." The snapshots tell a different story.

Miami City, 1995: This extraordinary home video shows an illuminated disc floating over a Miami suburb. Videotaped by a resident as it hovers just a few houses away, we watch as the craft dematerializes, in slow motion, right before our very eyes, frame by frame, down into a lightbulb-looking structure before disappearing altogether.

Some of the objects captured on this tape are truly "unidentified" in that they don't fit the typical description of a UFO. Cylinder-shaped objects, known as "probes," are captured on film scanning our shorelines and inspecting power lines, performing acrobatic maneuvers in mid-air while doing so.

Area 51, 1989: We can't keep away from this place, even though it's located in one of the most desolate expanses in the United States. Russian spy satellite photos from the '60s onward show the base has increased in size over the years. Amateur videos of the area taken at night show strange lights on radical test flights.

Perhaps the scariest footage of all is of the security forces that patrol the perimeters of Area 51 in unmarked jeeps and black helicopters, driving away unwanted onlookers. This "Best Known Secret Military Base" is located just off Highway 375, which was renamed "The Extraterrestrial Highway" in 1996 by the state of Nevada.

The "All-New Bob Lazar" on this videotape has Lazar opening up a little more about the "Dreamland" complex, telling us he saw nine ET saucers of various shapes and sizes. They were housed at the S4 site in a series of hangars carved into the mountainside. Upon seeing his first saucer, Lazar thought it was man-made until he entered the disc. He says on tape: "It's an ominous feeling. It feels as if you shouldn't be there. Not an exciting feeling. It brings up a whole lot of questions in your mind."

Lazar had to hang upside down to see into the lower level where the three large gravity amplifiers were located. They supposedly emitted the gravitational waves that propelled the craft. One amplifier was used to lift the craft up off the ground, and when all three were used, they formed the Delta

Configuration, creating a distortion to be used for space travel.

Lazar then adds a surprising thought: "When you're on the outside, you ask how could they keep something like this secret. It's a crime against science, it's a crime against people, but your feelings change once you're privy to the information."

Between pauses and gulps, Lazar surmises in concise sentences that the ET craft do exist. Something had to build them. So there must be aliens. And since he saw nine craft, there must be some sort of factory out there, meaning an entire civilization.

One of the most intriguing photographs on this video was of a religious painting found in one of the oldest churches in Russia. It depicts Jesus Christ hanging on the Cross, with two hovering discs in the background observing the crucifixion.

Mexico City, 1991: Possibly the largest mass UFO sighting in history, or at least captured on video. The sightings over the world's most populated city lasted almost an hour. Mexican officials had to finally hold a press conference, asking the public to remain calm as there were no reports of injuries or damage caused by the alien craft. Excellent photos of the bright objects in the sky were filmed from all angles. Citizens took an estimated two thousand hours of video.

Richard Hoagland
(Courtesy of Barbara Weaver)

In one striking sequence, with a clear blue sky as a backdrop, we watch a silvery metallic object traveling between two billowy white clouds when it stops in midair, reverses direction, then stops again to reverse direction and continue onward. What known aircraft can fly in this manner?

And then, the #3 video—*Hoagland's Mars: The NASA-Cydonia Briefings* (1991-83 min.). Finally I would get to see this famous video, the one that set the UFO community astir.

In 1988 and again in 1990, Richard Hoagland was invited by NASA to address several thousand of its scientists and engineers on the photographs taken by the 1976 Viking mission to Mars. This videotape is the filmed version of that presentation, complete with slides, on the series of structures that Hoagland claims are artificial, calculated, and prophetic.

Hoagland, a former science consultant to Walter Cronkite, is also the co-creator, with Carl Sagan, of Mankind's first interstellar message. Engraved upon a plaque, it was carried by Pioneer 10 beyond our solar system in 1971. It is intended to tell any extraterrestrials who may come upon the spacecraft or its remains where it came from and who sent it.

With his series of lectures, Hoagland was one of the first to promote NASA's photos of the Martian Cydonia region as actually showing a collection of artificial structures laid out in an extraordinary design. They had been taken in 1976 when two unmanned Viking spacecraft arrived at Mars. Their scientific objective: to determine whether there was life on the planet. The kind of life that NASA was looking for, however, would be microbiotic, and therefore not likely to be sending back messages.

As Carl Sagan put it, "Mars has surprised us."

What became controversial did not come from the Viking landers as they sat on the surface and collected soil samples, but from their orbital photographs. The Viking 1 orbiter had been looking for a suitable landing site for the second Viking craft,

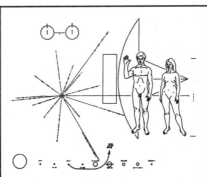

Mankind's first Interstellar Message showing the radio signature of our sun, where our planet is located, and what we look like (Courtesy of NASA)

when NASA scientists noticed a "face" carved into a mesa staring back at them on the fly-by.

In the twenty years since, NASA's official position is that the facial characteristics were simply a trick of light and shadow. Hoagland believes that NASA is simply exhibiting abject horror and fright that anything so outrageous could be real.

Hoagland's 3-D computer animation takes us gliding a few thousand feet above Martian surface, eventually arriving at the undeniable Face, estimated to be over a mile long and fifteen hundred feet high. When imaging processing is applied, this strange visage takes on details, such as teeth, two eye sockets, and a so-called hairline. This is not your average run-of-the-mill trick of light and shadow.

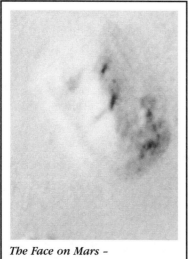

The Face on Mars –
looking familiar?
(Courtesy of NASA)

Looking down at the Face, one can see clearly the facial features are eerily suggestive of...dare we say it?...a monkey. In fact, Hoagland believes that it's a pretty good match to our own *Homo erectus*, a primitive anthropoid that lived on Earth around one-half million years B.C.

Hoagland reasoned that if the Face had a purpose, there might be other things nearby. He examined other photos of the Cydonia region and noticed a set of objects in what he terms "the city." Included in this city is perhaps the single most interesting object, the Face notwithstanding. It is a five-sided pyramid, important when you consider that five-sided objects do not form naturally.

The pyramid has two long sides, with the front angles connecting the three shorter sides at precisely 120 degrees. For Hoagland, this was essentially the breakthrough that lead to a stunning series of mathematical discoveries.

"Measurement is the beginning of a science," Hoagland tells us. "You do not have a science unless you can express it in numbers, finding numbers in constant not once, twice, but half a dozen times." Hoagland's investigation of life on Mars suddenly went from looking for footprints to a science of numbers. He believes that in the city's mathematics, there is an encoded message.

According to Hoagland, "Messages are defined as signals in the noise. How do you differentiate signals from the noise? Signals are redundant. What we have found are signals in a place you'd never suspect them, redundantly encoded not because they had nothing better to do, but because they may have been trying to tell us something. I say 'they' because something had to have placed these objects in this configuration."

Another interesting formation in the region is a crater that looks like it does not belong there. Unlike the other numerous craters dotting the surface of Mars, this one has a waterlogged look around its rim, as if water had splashed out and refroze in its wake. Just one more improbability taking place on this stark planet.

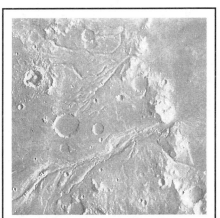

Martian channels – evidence that water may once have been abundant on the Red Planet? (Courtesy of NASA)

Mars today is an arid wasteland, but photographs taken by the Mariner 9 spacecraft (1972) revealed the "Red Planet" was once far different than as it appears today. Its features show signs of severe flooding, volcanic activity, and a north polar cap that seems to consist of frozen water.

What could this mean for those of us here on Earth? Is the

Face on Mars telling us something? As Hoagland suggests, maybe it's telling us that we may not quite be who we think we are. Perhaps it portends a possible future for Earthlings.

Or maybe this debate won't be answered until a scheduled NASA spacecraft lands on the planet in the year 2005, scoops up some more rocks and brings them back to Earth for analysis.

Until then, we'll have to be patient.

The fourth video on the list was *Flying Saucers Are Real!* (1993-50 min.). The tape is narrated by Stanton Friedman, the nuclear physicist who first discovered then investigated the leads that eventually led him to the Roswell UFO crash cover-up. He calls it the "Cosmic Watergate."

The Roswell Crash (July 2, 1947) is a slender thread of a story that has been retold many times, with few clues. Yet each ensuing year seems to see the leaking of more information about the "weather balloon" that allegedly crashed to the ground.

Interestingly enough, this saucer crash happened only days after America's first official UFO sighting, when a pilot named Kenneth Arnold reported seeing three saucer-shaped discs flying over the Cascade Mountains on June 24, 1947. The press coined the term "flying saucers" to describe what he saw, and it was the beginning of the modern UFO sightings phenomenon.

Stanton Friedman (Courtesy of Stanton Friedman)

According to Friedman, what the public in general does not know is that there were two separate crash sites found at Roswell, and that at this second site, at least one live alien was found.

In the book *Behold A Pale Horse* (Light Technology, 1991), the author writes that the alien found wandering dazed in the desert was referred to as an EBE (Extraterrestrial Biological Entity) because it had a different biological development from *Homo sapiens*. It was chlorophyll-based, processing food into energy in much the same way as plants.

A retired military guest on Art Bell's *Dreamland* claimed to have actually seen the dead alien bodies at Roswell. He affirmed that the bodies had no digestive system, no ears, and no vocal cords. They seemed cloned especially for space travel.

All the public knows for sure about Roswell is that one day the newspaper headlines were screaming, "RAAF Captures Flying Saucer On Roswell Ranch!" and the next day they were changed to read, "Crashed Weather Balloon Retrieved!"

And that's where the story lay until Friedman got involved in 1978. He talked to the town mortician who told him that local military base requested his smallest body bags. We hear about the base nurse who drew pictures of the "beings"—big heads on small bodies, four long slender fingers and no thumbs.

Of course, the question is: Where are these dead aliens now? And what happened to that live one?

Friedman ends the video by saying, "So they're holding back data. What does it matter? I think it matters a great deal. The best hope I see for a decent future for this planet is an Earthling orientation, instead of the nationalistic ones we grow up with. The easiest way to get to this Earth orientation is to recognize that to the aliens coming here, we are all Earthlings.

Our differences don't matter to them."

Ultimately, even for the believer, the Roswell story leaves us with deep suspicions. And no physical proof. The next step is up to the aliens, I guess.

The last video on this list was *UFOs: The Best Evidence—Vol 3* (1994-75 min.). The best evidence is evidently the UFO cover-up itself. The videotape begins by saying that the American taxpayer would have a fit if he knew where his some of his tax money was going, but since the so-called "Black Budget," from which our classified military programs are funded, has ballooned to $34 billion a year, we probably never will.

Studies prepared for NASA have predicted that a confirmed contact with a more advanced alien civilization would lead to the collapse and disintegration of human culture and institutions. The planet would be thrown into total chaos. The studies suggested that only a gradual indoctrination program would prevent this.

The Robertson Panel, however, submitted an analysis concluding that although UFOs were not a threat to national security, the continued reporting of UFOs could be a threat, and it recommended a policy of debunking flying saucers so that they would be stripped of their aura of mystery.

In the video segment called "Confrontations in Space," we see exciting footage taken in 1991 by the Space Shuttle Discovery of several objects floating along in the distance. Described by NASA as ice crystals, space debris, or both, one of the objects makes a sudden radical shift in direction and takes off at high speed in apparent response to a flash that emanates from the planet Earth. Moments later, we see what looks to be a missile fired in its direction. This sequence of frames suggests a hostile encounter between the NASA space agency and space junk.

The astronauts themselves appear to have the best stories to tell. Unfortunately, none of these courageous spacemen are willing to talk. In the book *Alien Bases On The Moon* (Steckling, 1981), the author writes that he believes our astro-

Russia's Mir Space Station against a backdrop of black space.

America's Space Shuttle Atlantis seen docking with Mir.

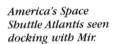

A view of the docking Atlantis from the Mir Space Station.

A successful docking of the Atlantis with Mir.

nauts follow in lock step and keep silent about their UFO encounters because they are trained to believe that it is in the best interests of national security.

Only one ex-astronaut, Gordon Cooper, certain that he had witnessed a UFO while flying a fighter plane over Europe, wrote a letter to the United Nations in 1978 stating so. Cooper has since recanted his statement but refuses to say what it was he saw or why he changed his mind.

Some astronauts have said that they would be willing to talk in an open forum about what they've seen and experienced, if they could be guaranteed that their careers and their families would not be in danger. Otherwise, they supposedly won't even speak about the subject with their spouses.

This videotape also relates that the Russians seem convinced that there were several encounters between ETs and American astronauts while on the moon. And the reason why the USA doesn't return to the moon is because they were told to stay away.

This video leaves us questioning why the U.S. Government is cowering away from the alien topic like a frightened child? And if it's true that Washington leaks like a sieve, why has this hole so effectively been plugged up?

Crawford invited me over to his Hollywood home for an interview. His apartment was warm and cozy (thanks to his wife), and decorated in an eclectic motif of African masks, Indian throw rugs, and gilded mirrors. A conga drum set up in the corner

Tim Crawford and author

added to the festivity. Crawford also plays in a jazz band.

I asked him how he got started in the UFO video distribution business.

> "About nine years ago," Crawford replied, "I was working in the video distribution industry, so I knew the business that way. Then one day a friend lent me the Bob Lazar and Richard Hoagland videos, and they blew me away. I realized that public TV was never going to show this stuff, so I went to a local UFO convention to seek out more tapes. Once there, I realized that there were hundreds of UFO videos and that the public was unaware of their existence. So this inspired me to start 'UFO Central.'"

You seem enthusiastic about your product.

> "I would sit down and view every single title that passed through my hands, and I started seeing strong scientific evidence of ETs. Every phenomenon must eventually pass the legitimacy of scientific theory and testing, and some of these tapes were sharing with us the results of this research."

So let us discuss the first tape—Bob Lazar and his *Excerpts From The Government Bible*.

> "There's the message, and then there's the messenger. First, we should consider: Is the message real? But, for some, there are doubts about Lazar's background. I believe that the technology he presents us far outweighs the uncertainly about his background."

Please discuss Richard Hoagland's *Monuments On Mars*.

> "This is another tremendous video. Hoagland did a excellent job of promoting the data that NASA has chosen to ignore. But we also can't forget the many original researchers, such as Carlotto, DiPietro, and

Molenaar because the most important thing about evidence is that it must first must be looked at, and these men did it first."

What do you make of the mathematical evidence found at the Martian ruins?

"What we have on Mars is ET archeology encoding higher-dimensional mathematics, also found in the Kabbalah and the King's Chamber in the Great Pyramid, which are both encoded books of Sacred Geometry. Mathematics is the one true language of the Universe."

What can you tell us about Stan Friedman and the Roswell crash cover-up?

"Friedman does a great job of making us aware of the technology we have today, and how fastly it has advanced. He also demonstrated how a civilian can use the legal system to gain access to secret Government documents that should now be available through the Freedom of Information Act."

I'm sure that most of America has by now seen the famous *Alien Autopsy* (1995). Was it a hoax?

"For me, the film fell short at its source. All of the evidence comes from the cameraman, but we never got to meet the person from whom this information came. I will also say that it could have been excellent special effects, but if it was staged, no one has come forward to claim it, so that, too, is amazing. There's just enough overall evidence to spin it into an intriguing mystery."

Now there's a video out called *The Alien Interview* (1997). It's the alleged interrogation of the alien that was found wandering in the desert at Roswell. According to the Art Bell Show, it's a 65-minute documentary that is "absolutely riveting," Bell believing it to be more than an interrogation, bordering on torture. The source of this material is a mystery person called "Victor," who smuggled out the film and has now gone into hiding. What's your take on this tape?

"Here again, we can't do anything but be spectators. As long as 'Victor' remains in hiding, we have to keep our ideas suspended and our opinions on the fence."

Tell us what you know about the crop circle phenomenon.

"I believe that some crop circles are of ET origin, and some are man-made, and that we're spectators in a great conversation between humankind and the stars."

Even the hoaxes?

"The question is, do these hoaxers know what they're doing?"

Crawford showed me some small photo albums on his coffee table that contained years of chronologically-arranged crop circle photos. Thumbing through the pages, one can see the formations growing more and more complex over the years.

I asked Crawford if he had ever seen a UFO.

"No, but in a sense, that's to my advantage. I'm grounded objectively in that I can stand back and look solely at the facts being laid out before us. And what I'm seeing makes me want to shout, 'Hey, all that stuff they're showing you on TV is distracting you from what's really going on!' I'm seeing research that's bringing a realness to the subject."

In this age of video cameras everywhere, why is it so hard to bring a realness to the subject?

"I've heard that there wouldn't be a UFO cover-up if the aliens didn't want it that way."

There's much literature being published today on "secret societies" that supposedly control our global Government. And I'm thinking that maybe it's the aliens themselves who control this whole global conspiracy thing.

"Conspiracies tend to me read like crime stories, with the criminal and the victims. I'm not sure there are any criminals here. But your statement has logic. If the aliens wanted us to know for certain they were here, they could do so."

Give some reasons why you believe UFOs would come here.

"I can see only three reasons for UFOs to be coming here: as missionaries, as conquerors, or as researchers. Unfortunately, history has shown that every contact between two cultures, no matter what the reason, has destroyed the lesser culture."

So we have the missionaries...

"In which case, if we use our own history as an example, the past suggests that the road to Hell is paved with the best intentions. And if they were here as conquerors, they would have done so long ago, as with every passing year, we get harder to take out."

And if they're here as researchers?

"From what I understand, the two dominant groups of aliens on this planet are the Pleiadeans, who look like us, and the Greys, with the big heads and wraparound eyes. The ones who make 'contact' with us are the Pleiadeans, who are spiritually-oriented entities, concerned about our well-being and the future of our planet. It's the Greys who are linked to the abduction phenomenon, who traumatize and cause confusion, but they apparently have the right to be here, and so the Pleiadeans can't stop them."

Does the increasing evidence of the possibility of ET-influenced genetics on Mankind influence your belief in a God?

"The ET genetics reinforces my belief in

God. I believe that the Universe is one great
Mind, and that God is the Higher Self of that
Mind. And that anything can and will take
place in that Mind. UFOlogy shows us where
science and religion are coming together."

And where does Tim Crawford stand today in his search for
the Truth?

"I'm just following a trail left by the question
'Was this Universe created by a Creator, or
just an accident?' And I believe there is a
design behind it all. We are an eternal spirit
life form, but we're so caught up in the dis-
tractions of material reality, we can't break
free from its constraints. [Crawford held up
a sheet of paper to show me the edges.] We
see ourselves as straight lines, but God [and
he turned the page front-wise toward me]
sees us as a full page, as our higher dimensional selves."

After our interview, I got to thinking: Let's assume that
because of the video camera, the world is gradually becoming
aware of the alien presence. The UFO secrecy veil has been
ripped, and information is now slowly trickling out. Perhaps
the U.S. Government itself is actually assisting in this by indoc-
trinating us to UFOs through movies, TV, and advertising. The
citizens of America appear to be ready.

My question is: Whatever happened to that live alien that
they found wandering in the desert, the one they took back to
the military base to interview? And why didn't his buddies
come back and rescue him?

If a picture is worth a thousand words, then these five
videos have left me speechless. But being left speechless does-
n't answer any questions. Fantastic footage? Absolutely. Spooky
possibilities? You bet. Hard evidence? There's the rub. In this
age of videotape, we have not one clean photo of an alien or a
close-up of his spacecraft.

The following week, I returned the Top Five videotapes to Crawford's Venice Beach warehouse and found his office as busy as ever. Phones were ringing off their hooks. Crawford was fast becoming known as the "UFO Answer Man." He'd done thirty radio interviews in the past three weeks. Like the rest of us, he's fascinated by what could be the biggest story of the Millennium. The questions that he was trying to answer: Where do we come from, and where are we going? And between these two unseens, what is reality?

Crawford took time out to allow his secretary to snap a picture of the two of us, and I grabbed a catalogue on my way out. His video company distributes over twelve hundred videos, and he's seen them all. He's more than the man with the film in the can. He's a man on a mission. That's good for us. He's our eye on the skies.

For a complete catalog listing of UFO
and paranormal audio and videotapes,
write to:
>   UFO Central
>   2321 Abbot Kinney Blvd.
>   Venice, California 90291
>
>   www.ufocentral.com

Chapter Eight

The Clones
Are Coming!

You know who they are –

you've heard all about them

they're the Men in Black

They're faceless, emotionless

clothed in superstition –

bathed in paranoia –

But don't let them scare you

just because they all look alike

The Clones
Are Coming!

You know who they are—the Men in Black. Government clones, perhaps soulless, perhaps mindless entities, being sent out by the Pentagon. It's an ongoing attempt to mass produce genetically-identical replicas of the originals.

Once perfected, NASA may send clones on long-distance space journeys. Today, however, these creatures are just beginning to learn to walk the Earth, perhaps marching us towards a New World Order, one ruled by a Global Dictator...

Don't let the above story scare you, but as Mankind watches the advance of cloning...two identical sheep...two identical monkeys...how long do you think it will be before you see one too many look-alike neighbors? Someday soon, Mankind is going to have to stop wondering—how far is too far?

By then it will be too late.

Every hard-working scientist is a dreaming Frankenstein, and for biogeneticists—the dream is coming alive! Who will be the first to achieve that long-sought status: Co-creator of human life with God? And imagine having a zombie-like entity doing your bidding. Large corporations and governments have. Maybe you won't be laughing when one or three of them come knocking at your door.

According to paranormal researcher Jim Keith, those who have had encounters with these Men in Black call them cold and very terrifying. Witnesses often use the word "sinister" in describing them. These MiBs have been described as not quite alien, not quite human, but a peculiar in-between.

And these Men in Black do have their habits. Apparently they like to travel in threes, and despite their reported pasty-white skin coloring, they prefer to dress in black from head to toe. Black hat, black suit, black shoes. Dark sunglasses.

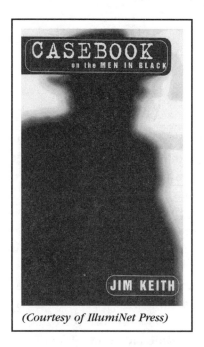

(*Courtesy of IllumiNet Press*)

"This subject is unlike any that I have written about," writes Keith in his book *Casebook on the Men in Black*, "and it quickly became apparent to me that it is almost impossible for the researcher to objectively grapple with these some-times ectoplasmic stranglings and their nightmarish doings. Their lore is too strange, their M.O. far too reminiscent of Bela Lugosi in his decline."

Keith's explorations into this shadowy and sometimes plain crazy phenomenon has brought up many interesting questions, such as whether the CIA or another government intelligence agency is instrumental in creating MiBs, or whether the project is privately financed. And, of course, is the military somehow involved? As one historian put it, the whole phenomenon is indicative of some kind of clandestine intelligence activity.

These "dark morphlings," as Keith calls them, have come to be associated with UFO sightings, and seem more concerned with the silencing of UFO witnesses than anything else. Witnesses say they sense a feeling of evil intent when these

MiBs arrive, often driving up in a black car, usually a Cadillac, although Keith notes, "In my British Men in Black files, the cases usually mention a Jaguar as their vehicle of choice."

Whatever their intent, the impression that they leave with their witnesses is one of—well, why not let some of them tell their own stories?

"A black, late model Cadillac pulled up in front of the house, and three very pale, very bald men in black suits got out. They moved rather slowly and methodically. They were stiff and emotionless, almost like robots."

Or "a thin man completely dressed in black stepped out from behind a shed. There was something, well, dead about him."

Or "he had a grey-toned face, and long tapering fingers. I felt he had a malevolent intent."

These MiBs are depicted as cold, emotionless and "the strangest looking men I've ever seen." Often their eyes bulge out like "thyroid eyes," and they are said to walk with exceptional slowness and care, like they're dazed or drunk. They are often mistaken for undertakers. Thick shoe soles are also frequently mentioned, presumably to add an inch or two to their height.

Another idiosyncrasy of these MiBs is that they share a language problem. They speak in slow monotones, using a sequence of words very evenly spaced, often with accents that can't be identified. All in all, they come off as extraterrestrial Mafiosi.

These strangers will threaten UFO

Photo of an alleged MiB standing in doorway (Courtesy of Timothy Beckley)

witnesses and their families, warning them not to discuss their UFO experience with anyone else: "We know what you have seen and we know that you have talked. An accident may happen to you if you say anything more about it."

"Then the man raised a camera, and took my picture." The flash gun is another recurring MiB detail (much like in the *Men in Black* movie of 1997). "His flash gun was very bright. It blinded me momentarily. He got in his car and drove off."

Or "I was fumbling for the light switch when he took my picture. There was a big flash and I couldn't see a thing."

Noting that flash guns seem to be used a lot to disable witnesses, Keith's research led him to a man named John Keel, the author of the now-classic *The Mothman Prophecies* (Dutton, 1975). The *Mothman Prophecies* is considered to be the first book on Men in Black, as Keel himself was personally harassed by MiBs over a period of time.

The book is also about "men with wings" and a series of strange sightings in the late 1960s. Keel concludes that his whole community (the Ohio River Valley) had served as a "test tube" for a psychological experiment on the populace. He suggests that it was conducted by the U.S. Government, probably privately financed, and involved the use of drugs, flash guns, and electronic visual effects.

At the end of his book, Keel writes: "The Air Force had lied to me. The telephone company lied to me. The UFO entities lied to me. My own senses, on occasion, had lied to me." And yet, one is left with the impression that Keel is ultimately a UFO skeptic.

Keith also points out these MiBs seem to share another very peculiar trait: no lips, or at best, ill-formed lips. This is reminiscent of a problem in cloning, where it's believed they still have trouble creating soft tissue. This could be why MiBs often appear Asian, with the soft eye tissue pulled too tight. Their lips are usually colored a bright red, as if painted on. They are also usually completely hairless, lacking even eyebrows and eyelashes.

Keith writes of a Dr. Herbert Hopkins who in 1976 claimed to have had an encounter with an MiB: "His skin was dead white, with an odd plastic consistency, and his lips were bright red. He was wearing gloves, and when he brushed his face, the red on his mouth was smeared. Then I could see that his mouth was perfectly straight. He did not have what we call lips, so the lipstick, I concluded, was some sort of decoy, only it was done poorly."

Hopkins relates how the MiBs did a disappearing coin trick, then told him that the same thing that happened to that penny happened to Barney Hill (the first nationally-known UFO abductee) because he talked too much.

When Keith told this story of Hopkins and the disappearing coin on Art Bell's *Dreamland*, Bell remarked, "Sounds like a mime." Keith replied, "Or a clone." Bell gasped.

And just how close are we to actually cloning a complete human being?

When interviewing Keith, he recommended that I read a book *In his Image: The Cloning of a Man* by David Rorvik (Dutton, 1978). The story is about the supposed first cloning of a human being, financed by a male individual described only as very wealthy and very influential.

At the time of the book's publication, in vitro, or test-tube, conceptions were very much in the news. Scientists around the world were still attempting to be the first to combine a human egg with sperm in a laboratory container, but it was already a highly-controversial procedure as far as ethics went: Could society and would society allow this "playing God" to take place?

Today, in vitro is a commonplace, if not a totally socially-acceptable, practice with more than half a million children around the world owing their lives to in vitro fertilization. As for human cloning, most researchers concede that it will come to pass whether society officially approves or not.

Rorvik writes: "Cloning is a process by which you could, without the union of two cells, reproduce a plant, an animal, or even a human being, and the offspring would be its genetic twin. The clone of a human would, of course, be a baby of the same sex."

And what would be some purposes for creating human clones?

For good or bad?

Good human clone usages would be to re-create beauty, or genius, or provide an infertile couple with a child. It could also rid our bodies of genetic disease, and even improve human performance by cloning individuals with "special effects," such as night vision or superb athletic ability. Or members of a common clone might be able to communicate intuitively with one another, helpful for deep water or deep space explorations.

And as for space travel, Rorvik writes: "On particularly long journeys to distant planets that we hope to explore and possibly colonize, a group of frozen human embryos would be included in the cargo. No need for cumbersome life-support systems or worries about getting bored. They could be thawed out, grown in test tubes, reared and instructed as to their missions in life by computer surrogates upon arrival."

Embryos might also be made readily available to the public from embryo banks, frozen and stored, then thawed out to be used as needed, animal or human, and free from all genetic defects. It's called "eugenics"—selective breeding. No sexual intercourse needed. Clients would not be in short supply.

Arguments against human cloning might include the possibility of re-creating a Hitler or his type, or creating "parahumans" for slavery purposes or to provide a ready supply of organs and limbs for medical use. This could mean that a parahuman could be killed without anybody being charged with murder. And if the body was cloned without a head, how could it say no?

Dolly the sheep, or 6LL3 as she was known in the lab, was the first adult mammal ever cloned, reproduced from the cell of an udder, hence she was named after Dolly Parton. She was genetically identical to the original sheep. But it all began with the first cloned carrot at Cornell University in the early 1960s, nurtured in a nutrient bath and developed into a full- fledged carrot. As one magazine put it: "In everyday language, they did something that most people consider to be science fiction."

And now that the science of cloning is here, Dolly will never go away again. And once human cloning gets started, despite all the laws and regulations, every possible use and mis-use will occur, just as "good men make good use of a neutral technology and evil men make evil use of it."

Animals which by all laws of nature should not exist can—and will—exist. There are many scientists who find this potential far more fascinating than repellent, more curious than frightening. This idea of mad scientists and their mutant misfits brings to mind the image of H.G. Wells' *The Island of Dr. Moreau*, where human DNA and animal DNA were spliced together in the laboratory to create monstrous hybrid creatures.

Today, they call these life forms "chimeras," from the mythological Chimera, which had the head of a lion, the body of a goat, and the tail of a serpent. A chimera is a crea-ture of mixed genetic heritage— various blends of

Possible chimera

human DNA, animal DNA, and plant DNA. This is one area of

scientific research that is totally unregulated, and the results are being patented as "inventions" or "machines."

The already-legendary "chupacabra," or goat sucker, is believed to be a very recent chimera. Rumored to be a group of clones that escaped from a South American experimental lab, they're said to resemble a kangaroo with a monkey head cloned onto it.

As for human cloning, the question then arises: Can a person's own consciousness survive the death of his (or her) body and be relocated into the body of a clone? In other words, would you retain your personality?

Dr. James Watson, co-discoverer of the DNA helix, saw human cloning something akin to the collapse of Western civilization. Overall, mass human cloning would be hard to resist. DNA from a popular figure could be worth a fortune on the black market. One scholar envisions a massive "war of the clones" in the future.

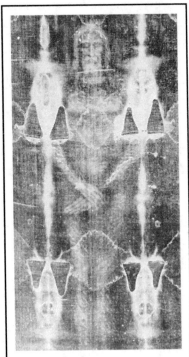

The Shroud of Turin – its DNA containing supernatural properties of Jesus? (Courtesy of Vernon Miller ©1978)

Another possibility to consider is the belief that the coming Antichrist—the Image of the Beast—will be a clone. A clone may have no reason to show Mankind any kind of mercy.

Scientists have even been discussing the possibility of extracting DNA from the Shroud of Turin and cloning Jesus, an intriguing idea in that the clone may contain the same supernatural healing abilities that Jesus possessed.

But we're not there yet. Or are we? Supposedly scientists still have trouble with soft tissue. Lip tissue is hard to form. So is the anus. What we do know is that each tiny cell of your body contains the entire genetic schemata of your brain, your mind, and, we assume, your soul.

"Well, perhaps not the soul," writes Rorvik. "Perhaps that's the one part of man you can never clone. Perhaps then, the uniqueness of each individual will thus always be preserved, even in a world of clones."

Perhaps.

So many questions still to answer, and science marches on anyway. According to Rorvik's book, somewhere in the world a human being cloned in a laboratory test tube has already celebrated his twenty-first birthday.

And so just who is behind this MiB phenomenon, this possible mass cloning of human beings?

Keith writes: "Are the Men in Black members of the CIA or some other intelligence agency? In some instances, that seems to be the probable case. Or are they extraterrestrial entities themselves? The reports are so bizarre that many of them defy any sort of Earthly explanation."

Keith also points out that even the Sasquatch, those hairy ape-men also known as Yeti and Bigfoot, have been known to show up in the vicinity of UFO sightings, so Bigfoot and Men in Black could be co-workers.

So should you see a group of three men, dressed alike in black suits and wearing dark sunglasses, walking in a stiff motion with soft tissue stretching their eyes too tight—ask to see their lips.

Or maybe this is no laughing matter. It is certainly one of our most perplexing mysteries. No one knows where these MiBs come from, or who they represent, and being dressed up in black suits, and black ties, and black sunglasses doesn't help any.

For now, however, let's just pretend they're hallucinations.

I was able to interview Keith in Reno, Nevada, by phone. He's written over a half-dozen books on the paranormal, and expresses much enthusiasm for the whole UFO phenomenon. He confided to me that he'd been studying UFOs since the 1950s. I asked him if he's ever seen a UFO.

Jim Keith
(Courtesy of Jim Keith)

"No, I haven't seen a UFO," Keith replied, "but the first intimation I have of being intrigued in the paranormal was about the age of six when I saw *The War Of The Worlds* at the movies. I was young, it was on the big screen, and it completely captivated me. I've been a sci-fi buff ever since, including the occult and UFOs and anything that wasn't mundane reality."

You wrote: "I had a terrifying experience with an alien in 1972 that seemed real enough to me." Care to elaborate on that?

"In 1972 [age 23], my close encounter was with a classic Grey, staring me in the face as I lay in my bed."

This would be years before Greys were classic.

"Exactly, and that lends credibility to the reality of the experience. Then fifteen years later, I see the Grey alien on the cover of Whitley Strieber's *Communion*, and when I read the book, his specific details exactly aligned with my experiences."

What kind of details?

"The color of the skin was not grey but blue-grey. And the texture looked to be a plasticine."

So then, Mr. Keith, are you an abductee?

"I don't really know. Certain things make me think that it's possible."

And what are your emotions about the Greys today?

"Oddly enough, I don't fear Greys, but the experience wasn't necessarily what I would have liked it to have been."

In your book *Black Helicopters Over America*, you write that these helicopters are often seen around cattle mutilation sights, either before or after, sometimes flying in military formation. What is the story behind cattle mutilations?

"It's a long story, because people associate cattle mutilations with UFOs. However, the experience of flying saucers being connected with mutilations—and all kinds of animals are being mutilated—is almost nil. What you do see is a lot of bright lights and black helicopters. The bits and pieces that we can nail down say terrestrial."

For example?

"A bacterial agent called 'clostridium' has been found on many of the carcasses, and many are marked with a fluorescent paint. Also, large pickup trucks are frequently spotted nearby. I believe it to be a cover-up for bio-warfare testing."

This all makes for great science fiction.

"Technology has turned into science fiction at every level. Our world is sci-fi today. We've broken down the barrier between the realms of science and fantasy."

You've written a number of books about cover-ups [*The*

Octopus, Okbomb!, and *The Gemstone File*]. They basically say that a select number of people—the rich elite—rule the world (with Aristotle Onassis being this century's #1 culprit, involved in everything from kidnapping Howard Hughes to killing JFK). It all sounds so entangled that it soon appears convoluted. Where do you draw the line in terms of a story's credibility?

> "A conspiracy by definition is incredible with some of its details, so that's the nature of the beast. I sit down and try to prove the propositions to myself by trying to sort them out. But a conspiracy tends to be radical, and protected by the fact that it is incredible. People don't believe that the incredible exists."

How does one go about researching a conspiracy?

> "I attack the topic in any manner I can. I'll look everywhere. And my most valuable resource is the many researchers and contacts that I've made around the world. I get in touch with them, and when I get all the material in, whether by mail or by phone, I go over it and try and put it all together. I'll also make the occasional foray to the library."

And where do you stand on the conspiracy issue today?

> "I'm at an interesting crossroads in my life right now, and I'm not even sure I'm comfortable talking about it. I've engaged myself in the study of conspiracy theories for a number of years now, and I find that I'm getting more into the philosophy, rather than the nuts-and-bolts, behind conspiracies."

Such as?

> "Such as 'why do we even exist in a world that has a weave of conspiracies running through the fabric of our planet?'"

What do you believe to be the foremost conspiracy going on in the world today?

> "I believe that would be the conspiracy to

be human. We are continually being reminded of our own finite character, of our animal
desires, of our limitations, as in 'it's human to
err,' and that we are not transcendent beings.
We are being bombarded by all this negativi-
ty, and I believe that might be a strategy for
this 'elite,' as you called them, to maintain
their control."

Near the end of your book, you write: "Reality is a conven-
ient fiction invented to reassure us that the deck will remain
under our feet within an infinitely strange Universe." Did any
one thing shake you up enough to cause you to question the
stability of the ground upon which you stood?

"No one thing. It seems to me that my whole
life has been spent walking on that path. I
do believe that the bottom line of reality is
that it is a dream."

Is there a Creator at the bottom of this dream-like reality?

"I believe so."

And what is your concept of this God?

"My concept of God is of One God, so that
when I imagine a separation between myself
and this Great Oneness, I believe I am cutting myself off from that reality. I don't
believe in two things in the Universe. I
believe there is only One Principle."

Keith's book paints a frightening picture of a possible
future to come. Those lurid tales of human and animal cloning
that were once the property of science fiction are now fast
becoming fact. And I understood what he meant about trying
to gather all of your notes together and make some sense of it
all. If only we could sort together the pages of our lives, maybe
there would be a clue in there somewhere as to just where we
are headed.

And I can't help but think about those Men in Black standing outside my window tonight, beneath the streetlamp in the

pouring rain. Dressed in their black raincoats, hats pulled low to keep the rain off their faces, but still getting soaked to the bone. And having no real place to call home. Their painted-on lips are undoubtedly melting in the rainfall, but it doesn't matter. They have no mothers or fathers to kiss them with anyway.

Are human clones to be creatures like you and I, talking and laughing and sharing our living space? Or will they feel alienated and aloof from the human race?

Like us, perhaps they will feel a little of both.

Casebook on the Men In Black
(IllumiNet Press, 1997)
        Jim Keith

In His Image: The Cloning of a Man
        David Rorvik (Dutton, 1978)
        is out of print, but enquire
        at your local library.

For a listing of books and tapes, write to:
        IllumiNet Press
        P.O. Box 2808
        Lilburn, Georgia 30048

Chapter Nine

The Interlocutor

You're taking down names

and getting photos

when suddenly

You find that you're a ringmaster

of the supernatural –

are you crazy?

As a master of ceremonies of the

paranormal – that's a given

The Interlocutor

Pursue the paranormal, and you're dealing with mystics, where the business side of things tends to get blurry, and proofs can vanish. Publishing can make for strange enough bedfellows, but throw in a cast of arcane characters under the covers and you're bound come up with some pretty good tales. Cloaked in a fog of paranoia and basic mistrust, perhaps, but the stuff from which legends are woven.

Someone who's done business in this murky literary world for over thirty years is Timothy Green Beckley. His Inner Light Publications was one of the country's first New Age publishing houses, established back when paranormal wasn't cool, or at least, as Beckley would put it, not profitable. He has since published such highly-respected New Age authorities as Brad Steiger, John Keel, and T. Lobsang Rampa. Beckley doesn't like to play it up, but he's considered an old-timer; an achievement, considering that all things mystical have a tendency to disappear as in a puff of smoke.

In the course of his career, Beckley's promoted everything from rock concerts to boxers, and once worked as a stringer for the *National Enquirer*. He's authored over thirty books, written for over forty magazines, and presently edits the

Timothy Green Beckley (circa 1972) (Courtesy of Inner Light Publications)

nationally-distributed *UFO Universe* magazine.

To speak to Beckley would be to hear straight from the horse's mouth about the behind-the-scenes and the business side of UFOs. I was anxious to hear what this publishing old-timer had to say.

I contacted his office in New York, and he returned the call. He's enthusiastic. He's cynical. And he was resplendent with tales of mysterious characters on all sides of the ocean. On my end of the phone, I laughed a lot. Beckley is gregarious with a quick turn of a phrase.

Beckley started out as a rock music critic, and over the decades, he has had the opportunity to quiz the rich and famous on a variety of matters, and because of his own personal interest in UFOs, there has hardly been an occasion when the subject hasn't popped up.

"At one point in my varied editing career," writes Beckley in his book *UFOs Among The Stars*, "I was probably writing thirty articles a month on whoever was the big rock band or teen favorite at the moment. Some of the musicians I spoke with on the subject are dead serious about UFOs, while others take these things more lightly."

Case in point: Jimi Hendrix.

Beckley can't honestly say that he knew Jimi Hendrix, but after watching Hendrix give one great performance after another in the New York area, Beckley somehow managed to wind up backstage at an outdoor rock festival held on Randales Island in the early '70s.

"As I recall, Hendrix was leaning up against a wall of amps and speakers," writes Beckley. "As I walked past him, we both nodded as if we recognized each other, and to this day I can swear I heard him ask me, 'And what planet are you from, pal?'"

Hendrix, of course, went on to become one of the legendary guitarists of the rock era. At the same time, many of his audience found his manner of dress and lifestyle confusing, as if he had come from elsewhere and stepped into an earthly body. Beckley hypothesizes that this may have been because

(Courtesy of Inner Light Publications)

Hendrix fits perfectly some of the characteristics of a "walk-in."

A walk-in is defined as the blending of one spirit with another, both sharing the same physical body. The difference between being possessed by an evil spirit and a walk-in is that the walk-in has complete permission by the original human spirit. These people are quite different from the average individual, and may easily be viewed as misfits in the physical world.

After Hendrix's death in 1970, Beckley befriended musician Curtis Knight, a fellow bandmate of Hendrix and a good friend from the early days. Knight told Beckley: "What is not generally known is that Jimi expressed a great interest in matters of an extraterrestrial nature, and admitted to numerous UFO sightings. Hendrix even once told a reporter from the New York Times that he was really from Mars." According to Knight, Hendrix wasn't kidding, either.

On several occasions, UFOs would show up while Hendrix was giving a concert. Near the end of his career, he performed a concert on the rim of an extinct volcano in Maui, retiring into a sacred Hopi Indian tent between sets. UFOs were sighted all over the volcano area, people were calling in to a local radio show to report the sightings, and a cameraman supposedly nearly fainted after sighting a UFO through his camera lens.

Knight knew all about the UFO episode over Maui: "Jimi felt certain the UFOs had come down to put their spiritual stamp of approval on the show. He told me that he'd been emotionally and physically recharged by the experience."

Hendrix's interplanetary interest can be seen in his music. Many of his song lyrics contain veiled references to UFOs, and in the film *Rainbow Bridge*, Hendrix talks for several minutes about astral projection and the philosophy of the Space Brothers. His album *Axis: Bold As Love* opens with an announcement about flying saucers, followed by a catchy song called "Up From the Stars."

Hendrix has now passed from this physical plane. But if it is true that he was a walk-in, the question now remains: Where did he walk out to?

Beckley first met David Bowie because of a mutual acquaintance with a woman named Wallie Elmlark, who was a practicing white witch. Elmlark was a regular speaker at the New York School of Occult Arts and Science, one of the country's first New Age centers, which Beckley founded during the late '60s. "This was during the time David was going through his metaphysical stage," writes Beckley. "David would often consult Wallie on career moves and more private situations, since she had a reputation for being a highly 'sensitive' individual. It was during this period that Bowie became known for his onstage portrayal of an extraterrestrial being by the name of Ziggy Stardust. Together with his band The Spiders From Mars, Bowie created a sensation wherever he appeared."

"I'm very much interested in science fiction, " Bowie told Beckley during a chat in a Manhattan RCA recording studio. "I've always been fascinated with the idea that life might exist elsewhere in the universe, and the possibility that space beings might be traveling to Earth."

Beckley discovered that as a youth in England, Bowie

helped put together a UFO magazine. Bowie claimed that the entire magazine's staff had frequent sightings of sometimes as many as five or six craft at a time: "They would come over on a regular basis to the point where we could time them. Sometimes they just stood still, while other times they moved about oh so fast that it was hard to keep a steady eye on them."

Among Bowie's biggest selling hits include titles such as "Space Oddity" (about an astronaut lost in space), and "Starman" (dealing with an alien's visit to Earth). But Beckley also discovered that Bowie was hesitant to discuss his paranormal experiences, fearing the media is always looking to sensationalize his every move. Beckley reports, however, that there are those among Bowie's close followers who contend that the rock star has actually experienced some sort of contact with otherworldly beings.

And Bowie did jump at the chance to play the starring role in the sci-fi cult film *The Man Who Fell to Earth*, the saga of an extraterrestrial (like Ziggy Stardust, or perhaps Bowie himself), who has crashed to Earth in a flying saucer, and finds it impossible to fit into society.

Beckley spoke to John Lennon twice, once backstage at a rock concert that Beckley had promoted, and again on the telephone when a mutual friend had connected the two so that Lennon could relate to him his telepathic experience.

Beckley was doing an article on a faith healer when he discovered that Lennon had befriended the healer and had invited him over to his apartment in the historic Dakota building near Central Park. Over the phone, Lennon wanted to confirmed to Beckley that the psychic did indeed have a gift: "One night Yoko and I watched as he made some candies wrapped in cellophane just jump out of a candy dish and move across the table until they landed on the floor. At no time did he touch them."

It was soon after that telephone conversation that Lennon and May Pang, his live-in girlfriend, saw a UFO. Beckley contacted Pang after Lennon's death, and found her happy to share her remembrances about one of the greatest legends of our time.

May Pang holds her prized photo of John Lennon pointing to the spot in the sky where they sighted the UFO (Courtesy of Inner Light Publications)

Beckley writes: "'John was always fascinated with the unusual,' May explained, handing me his once-treasured copy of the *I Ching* that she still has on her library shelf. 'He was always caught up in his fate, his destiny. He was, it seems, trying to understand his greatness and the impact he had on millions growing up in a very confused, almost lost generation.'"

Beckley notes that Lennon admitted in one interview to having a particular fascination with psychic phenomena as a kid:"I used to literally trance out into the alpha. I didn't know what it was called then. I found out years later that there is a name for those conditions. But I would find myself seeing hallucinatory images of my face changing and becoming cosmic and complete. It caused me to always be a rebel."

Pang was able to give Beckley the "scoop" on Lennon's Big Apple UFO encounter because she was there at his side during the incident:"We had just ordered up some pizza and since it was a warm evening we decided to step out onto the terrace. There are no windows directly facing us, so John just stepped outside with nothing on in order to catch a cool breeze coming across the East River. I remember I was just inside the bedroom getting dressed when John started shouting for me to come out on the terrace."

When Pang stepped out beside him, she saw the enormous

circular UFO. She and Lennon stood there mesmerized, unable to believe what they were seeing. She estimated it to be about the size of a Lear Jet and says that it was close enough to hit with a rock. The object passed from view, but soon returned. Lennon and Pang set up a telescope, and they managed to take some pictures, but the lights coming from the craft were so bright that the photos came out overexposed.

"We even called the police," said Pang, "that's how excited we were, and they told us to keep calm, that others had seen it too. All night long, John kept saying, 'I can't believe it...I can't believe it...I've seen a flying saucer.'"

John later used what he saw as part of the cover art on his *Walls and Bridges* album. Pang says that Lennon always had an interest in UFOs: "He even used to subscribe to a British UFO magazine, the *Flying Saucer Review*. But after seeing what we saw that night, he became even more fanatical, bringing up the subject all the time."

Not only musicians are touched by UFOs. Take, for example, the case of Jackie Gleason.

"Way back in the mid-1960s," writes Beckley, "I got a letter in the mail from Jackie Gleason Productions, Hollywood, Florida, ordering a copy of a mimeographed booklet I had put together relating to UFOs. To me, this was confirmation of what I had heard rumors about for a long time—that 'the Great One' was personally involved in researching UFOs. Supposedly, and I've since found out that this is true, Gleason had one of the largest UFO and metaphysical libraries in private hands. The collection of thousands of volumes was known to stretch from floor to ceiling and included numerous rare titles."

Gleason had good reason for his belief. He had twice sighted UFOs, and openly talked about them in public. But his obsession with them had an even deeper source. Gleason claimed to have actually seen the bodies of several aliens who died when their craft crashed in the American Southwest. And while the story was first revealed by Gleason's ex-wife Beverly to the *National Enquirer*, it had never been verified until

Beckley spoke with a young man, Larry Warren, who heard the story directly from Gleason's lips.

Warren was an Airman First Class stationed at Bentwaters NATO Air Base in England during an incredible Christmas week of 1980. A UFO landed and parked just outside the perimeter of the base in a dense forest.

"On the first of several nights of confrontation with the Unknown," writes Beckley, "three security police ventured into the area and came across an eerie-looking object hovering just above the ground. One of the MPs was mesmerized by the UFO and was unable to move for nearly an hour. While in this mental state, he received some sort of telepathic message that the craft would return. For the next few nights, up to eighty U.S. servicemen, British bobbies, as well as civilians from near-by farms, witnessed an historic event. According to Larry Warren, who stood within feet of this craft from another world, three occupants came out of the ship and actually communicated with a high ranking member of the U.S. Air Force."

"Jackie Gleason was interested in hearing my story first-hand," Warren told Beckley, explaining how he met the famous comic in May of 1986. Warren had been given a message that Gleason would like to talk with him privately, so a meeting was set for a Saturday at Gleason's home in Westchester County, New York, where Gleason would have time to relax and talk.

After being formally introduced, Gleason took Warren into his recreation room, complete with pool table, a full-sized bar, and hundreds of UFO books on the shelves lining the walls. Warren recalls discussing Gleason's previous UFO sightings, and the mystery of the Bermuda Triangle, but it wasn't until they'd each had a few drinks that Gleason began to loosen up and told Warren his stunning story.

"It was back when Nixon was in office," Gleason explained. "We were close golfing buddies and had been out on the golf course all day when somewhere around the 15th hole, the subject of UFOs came up. Not many people know this, but the President shares my interest in this matter, and has a large collection of books in his home on UFOs just like I do. For some reason, however, he never really took me into his confidence about what he personally knew to be true, one of the reasons being that he was usually surrounded by so many aides and advisers."

Later that night, however, Gleason received the surprise of his life when Nixon showed up at his house around midnight, all alone. No secret service agents were with him. Nixon told him that he wanted to take him someplace and show him something.

Gleason got into Nixon's car and they drove to nearby Homestead AFB (Miami, Florida): "I remember we got to the gate and this young MP came up to the car to look inside, and his jaw seemed to drop a foot when he saw who was behind the wheel."

They were allowed to proceed, and Nixon drove to the far end of the base where they stopped near a well-guarded building. Security allowed them to enter the structure, and Nixon took Gleason into a room where he pointed out what he said was the wreckage from a flying saucer. Nixon then took him into a second room where, according to Gleason, "there were six or eight of what looked like glass-topped Coke freezers. Inside them were the mangled remains of what I took to be children. Then, upon closer examination, I saw that some of the other figures looked quite old. Most of them were terribly mangled as if they had been in an accident."

Gleason recalled that the beings were about three feet tall, with grayish-colored skin and deep-set slanted eyes. And they definitely were not human, of this he was certain. Gleason said that all-in-all, it was a very pathetic sight. The President even had tears in his eyes. Warren asked if they could have possibly been from the wreckage from the crash at Roswell, New Mexico, but Gleason didn't know.

"For weeks following his trip with Nixon to Homestead AFB," Warren told Beckley, "the world-famous entertainer couldn't sleep and couldn't eat. Jackie told me that he was very traumatized by all this. He just couldn't understand why our government wouldn't tell the public all they knew about UFOs and space visitors. He said he even drank more heavily than usual until he could regain some of his composure and come back down to everyday reality. You could tell he was very sincere. He took the whole affair very seriously, and I could tell that he wanted to get the matter off his chest, which was why he was telling me all of this."

As far as Warren is concerned, he agrees with the Great One in that the U.S. Government needs to "come clean, stop lying to the public, and release all the evidence they have about these space visitors." Maybe then, we'll all be able to see the same things the late Jackie Gleason did. And Gleason reached the conclusion that extraterrestrials have arrived on our cosmic shores.

"Of all the famous folks I've spent time with discussing UFOs and theories about extraterrestrial civilizations," writes Beckley, "no one seems to know more about the subject, at least from a firsthand point of view, than retired heavyweight boxing champion Muhammad Ali."

Beckley first met the world's most famous prizefighter one morning around 5:00 A.M. Ali was sprinting along the trails leading through Manhattan's Central Park. His trainer, Angelo Dundee, had warned Beckley that Ali wanted to talk and jog at the same time. Ali had been working out in the park on a previous morning when he claimed to have sighted not one, but two UFOs moving over New York City.

Tim Beckley (far right) watching over Muhammad Ali's shoulder as he views UFO slides (Courtesy of Inner Light Publications)

"A number of reporters traveling with the Champ jumped on the story," writes Beckley, "and it was picked up by the wire services, though Ali was concerned that these reports made it sound as if the subject were to be treated as a joke. Ali wanted to let me know right from the starting bell that he was quite serious about what he had seen."

Ali revealed to Beckley that he'd had a total of sixteen sightings to date, and by the end of their conversation, Ali decided that he trusted Beckley enough to invite him back to his hotel room to talk further on the subject.

When Beckley arrived, Ali was flat on his stomach getting a rubdown from an aide while talking a mile a minute to a group of reporters gathered around him. Upon seeing Beckley, Ali said, "You know those objects we discussed in the park? They've been watching me for some time."

The reporters went crazy with the questions.

Beckley writes: "Ali's voice shifted to a more confidential tone, saying 'I don't like to talk about this much but we all seem to be open-minded here. One day, walking through the Florida Everglades, I saw this ship land and, as I watched, a door slid open and a ramp projected itself onto the ground. Out stepped a human-looking figure more than seven feet tall who proceeded to walk down the ramp and stand in front of me. Muhammad, he said to me, you will beat Sonny Liston!'

"The room filled with laughter. What had sounded at first like an honest account was really another of Ali's famous put-ons. 'Be sure to call me at home,' Ali said to me, grasping my hand into which he placed a slip of paper with his phone number. 'Come down and bring some photos, slides, film, anything you have on saucers, okay? I'll even tell you what they are, if you're interested enough.'"

Beckley was interested enough, and recalls being in awe upon finding himself and a couple of friends driving down the long, cobblestone driveway leading to the front door of Ali's estate in Cherry Hill, New Jersey.

"Hey, here are my UFO men!" Ali greeted them when they arrived. He wanted to know what they had brought with them. Beckley explained that he had brought along some film of flying saucers taken in West Virginia.

"At Ali's request," Beckley writes, "we ran the film three times while he pointed out the physical characteristics on these video saucers that were similar or identical to the ones he observed in real life. When we completed the screening, Ali asked if we could have copies made for him. 'I'd like to show them at my college lectures. UFOs tie in with what my teacher Elijah Muhammad says.'"

Indeed, such mystical matters as UFOs are a part of the religious teachings of the late Elijah Muhammad, founder of the Nation of Islam. Beckley writes that Ali produced a copy of the book *Message to the Black Man of America*, and read to him from a chapter titled "The Battle in the Sky is Near," which talked about the biblical vision of Ezekiel's wheel in the sky, and how Ezekiel's vision has become a reality.

Elijah Muhammad's follower, Louis Farrakhan, has gone on record saying that he has communicated with aliens. In October of 1989, at the Marriott Hotel in Washington, D.C., the religious leader told an audience of 10,000 that in 1985 he'd had a vision of being abducted by extraterrestrials and carried over Mexico in a spacecraft called the "Mother Wheel."

He wrote about it in *The Washington Post*, stating how the spacecraft brought him back to Earth and dropped him off near Washington to make an announcement. His announcement was that he had gotten the idea for the Million Man March while aboard the UFO.

Beckley spoke to Ali once again, this time at his training camp in Pennsylvania. Ali told Beckley that he was finding it a lot easier to live with UFOs than ever before: "I always speak my mind, since I found out that so many other people have had similar sightings. I've spent a lot of time in the last few years lecturing to college campuses around the country and I find students are open-minded towards the existence of things like this. I hope others will listen in the future as I am convinced UFOs are of tremendous importance to the whole world."

Beckley was once invited to speak before the members of the British Parliament. He'd been summoned to the House of

Lords by the Earl of Clancarty, who was part of a group pressing to get the British government to end its silence on the matter of UFOs. The Earl, Mr. Brinsley Le Poer Trench, was leading the push for those in positions of power to reveal what they knew to the British public.

"After my presentation," writes Beckley, "made in a secluded chamber within the honored halls of the House of Lords, I was invited back

Earl of Clancarty (Courtesy of Inner Light Publications)

to the Earl's London estate for dinner, and what started out to be light conversation, ended up as a serious discussion."

Beckley: How did you start to get the ball rolling on the question of UFOs in the House of Lords?

Earl of Clancarty: I took my seat in June, 1976. I started sounding a few of the other Lords out and found that quite a number were interested in the topic. In our country, if you want to find out something from one of our leaders, you can put it in writing or ask a question in the chamber. If you do both you must get a double answer. My questions led me to believe that there was a cover-up here in this country.

Beckley: What do you think the British government knows?

Clancarty: I'm sure they've got records of reports going back any number of years. What we want to do is to get material released. The whole thing is, we haven't got what you have in the U.S., a Freedom of Information Act. So we can't sue the intelligence department or the military or whatever it is. What we can do is get the government to come clean. I'm sure they've got plenty of reports. There are reasons for the cover-up. The original one, I think, has to do with panic, but also a number of countries might be trying to get hold of an alien spacecraft in operational condition, or in good order, not a crashed, smashed one.

Beckley: Do you think the British government has a crashed UFO?

Clancarty: It's possible, but I wouldn't know. I couldn't give you a good answer to that one. But I think that if one country were to get hold of one and were actually able to make more of them, that particular country would rule the world. That, of course, is the reason that a particular government would have a cover-up. Another possible reason for the cover-up is, that I think the government is aware of, is that aliens have bases on the Earth from which they operate and watch us.

Beckley: You were one of the first to write about extraterrestrials in ancient history. You found a lot of references in in the Bible, in Genesis.

Clancarty: Yes, indeed, Elijah was taken up in a whirlwind. All of the countries have their traditions of what we now call UFOs, for thousands of years. The Chinese and Japanese, South Americans and Hopi Indians, the Scandinavians and the Celts, all have them in their traditions. They [ETs] are concerned about us because they put us here. There are thousands and thousands of advanced civilizations in this galaxy that are communicating with each other. That would help to explain the different races that we have here on this planet, including the yellow, the red, white and the black. I think that many of them have come here from different civilizations and helped to colonize this planet. I think that they are basically friendly.

In the course of Beckley's journalistic career, he's interviewed celebrities from Buddy Rich to Tiny Tim to Dick Gregory, always asking his UFO questions. It was now his turn to provide some answers. We spoke by phone as Beckley sat in his New York office. I asked him if he had ever personally sighted a UFO.

"I was ten years old when I had my first UFO sighting," replied Beckley. "I was standing on the front porch of my parents' house in New Jersey, and watched two bright objects, circling and rotating. The next day, the paper said that other people had seen it, too. Even at the toddler age of ten, it was obvious to me that they were intelligently controlled. I wrote a letter to the local paper, and the local

Tim Beckley holds his prized photo of author pointing to his favorite guitar

radio station called me for an interview. Ever since then, I've been intrigued with the subject, and I've traveled extensively to gather facts about this global phenomenon. I've had two other UFO sightings since."

How did you get into publishing?

"At age fourteen, I published a small newsletter called *Interplanetary Newspaper Report*. Jim Moseley was publishing *Saucer News*, he contacted me, took over my subscriptions, and made me his editor. He's one of the original UFO researchers, going back to early fifties. I started self-publishing in the mid-sixties."

You've been in the UFO business for a good number of years. As a paranormal researcher, what has scared you the most?

"Some clown who wants a couple thousand dollars for a photograph. He must be clowning around because he's not getting a dime."

That does sound scary.

"Half the people in the UFO business are
pompous with their heads up their [arse].
You can quote me on that. Only exchange
the word ass with arse."

I told Beckley of my own self-publishing efforts and my
quest for pictures. I was trying to get an aerial photograph of
Area 51, but since the U.S. Government won't acknowledge the
place exists, how can they send me one? I need to give them
exact longitude and latitude. Where's my best chance of obtaining an aerial photo of "Dreamland?"

"The Russian Embassy." [See photo, Chapter
Seven]

You told me something curious, how you once promoted
the brother of Dr. Frank Stranges [see Chapter One] as an evan-
gelical preacher on the Bible Belt circuit throughout the South.

"His brother was a career evangelist, a holy
roller, all hellfire and brimstone. They would
bring out the piano and play and sing, and
then they would roll around on the floor
and talk in tongues. Frank could have been a
successful preacher on the circuit, too. But
Frank met his alien Commander Val Thor and
his whole mission changed."

Who's your most memorable interview?

"Muhammad Ali. He can just talk and talk
and talk for hours. He's very friendly and
upbeat, very sociable. And he treats everyone
as an equal, very unlike the persona he dis-
plays in the ring. He doesn't speak down to
people. He treats all races and creeds the
same. I think he's one of the great humani-
tarians of our time."

Tell your readers a favorite story from your days as a critic
on the rock music scene.

"I can think of a couple, but they're too

raunchy to repeat for your book. One
involved these two girls backstage...but
that's for a different kind of book."

Throughout your years of research, have you come across
any evidence of a UFO cover-up?

"UFOs have a way of covering themselves
up. And I believe the Government doesn't
tell what it knows because its too confusing,
too mind-blowing, encompassing too many
different avenues. Most military people don't
even know what's going on because they
aren't privy to the information. As for the
scarcity of evidence, I believe it's the ETs
themselves who don't want to be known."

Okay, Mr. Beckley, you and I are driving down the road, late
at night, radio turned on low, and a flying saucer lands on the
road ahead of us. Before we can grab a video camera, we're
being uplifted into a spacecraft, vehicle and all. Once we're
inside, safe and secure onboard, what would be your first question?

"Where's the men's room? I'm sure I'd be
ready to pee in my pants."

No trusting in a grand scheme of Creation?

"I'm a borderline agnostic."

So your concept of the Creator of this Universe is...?

"A Creator? I doubt it."

You see no spirituality behind UFOs?

"I do think there's a spirituality behind
them. Other creations and other realms is in
itself a spirituality. But that belief and a belief
in a Creator are for me two different ball-
games."

Then what about your long career spent investigating
UFOs? What do you think the whole phenomenon is all about?

"It's about a lot of different things. I think
our concept of reality needs to be drastically
changed. I don't think that our reality is nec-

essarily the correct one, nor do I think that
reality is a consistent. I always tell people
that UFOs act independently of what you or
I think."

Somewhere in Beckley's writings I read that it's impossible
to pin down an exact definition of UFOs. UFOs used to be
something that landed in a field. They're so much more now—
they're mystical, and spiritual, but also technical. They also tell
us that our Universe doesn't end here on Earth. And with the
stars above a million deep, it would be hard to argue that.

There are an estimated 200 billion stars in our galaxy, and
we are starting to detect the presence of planets around these
suns. And there are literally millions of other galaxies now
being found with the Hubble telescope. The chances of other
life existing somewhere out there is increasing. Our Universe
seems to be expanding.

As for the truth of these celebrities' claims, only you can be
the judge. Is our destiny written in the "stars"?

I liked Beckley's cynically optimistic take on life. He
advised me that in publishing, as in anything, the future is up
for grabs. Everything's negotiable, don't let 'em scare ya, and
whatever you're selling, promote it like a humbug. The bigger
the humbug, the better they like it.

His initial reaction to my telling him that I was about to
self-publish was an inaudible cheer that came out sounding like
a nostalgic sigh. Throughout our interlocution, he never told
me no but simply laid the facts out bare and let me decipher
the meaning. I liked what I saw.

So did Beckley. The world of paranormal publishing is a
path he's pursued for over three decades, and he says he
wouldn't trade a supernatural minute of it. Well, maybe there
are a couple of times he'd like to turn back the clock, but as far
as my book was concerned, he advised me to do a quality job,
then wait until doomsday to get paid.

I'm willing to do the first.

UFOs Among The Stars
(Inner Light Publications, 1992)
        Timothy Green Beckley

For a listing of books and tapes, write to:
        Inner Light Publications
        Box 753
        New Brunswick, New Jersey 08903

        www.webufo.net

Chapter Ten

The Cosmic Host

He turned his alien abduction

into a heart-stopping novel

The large-headed Grey alien

on the cover struck a nerve

Millions of people – worldwide

picked up that cover

But it was the story inside

that truly frightened them

The Cosmic Host

Perhaps Whitley Strieber has a powerful storytelling ability to make the unreal seem real. At the time that his odyssey began, he was already a well-known horror writer (*The Hunger*, *The Wolfen*), specializing in imaginative thrillers. This led many of his critics to believe that his novel *Communion* was a work of fiction, and that trying to pass it off as a true story was a fraud.

How does one begin, then, to tell a tale so horrifying that you know it will be disbelieved, perhaps most strenuously by those who desperately don't want it to be true? The very first page warns: When you read this incredible story, do not be too skeptical. Somewhere in your own past there may be some lost hour.

For Strieber, it began in December of 1985 when one night he suddenly awoke to a peculiar whooshing sound coming from the living room downstairs. He listened with "an edge of fear," and when he saw one of his bedroom doors opening, his heart started pounding.

The "visitor" that appeared in the doorway was about three and a half feet tall, wearing a hood so that its face could not be seen. Strieber remembers that he took no action. He believes that his mind was already under some sort of control. The next thing he knows, the figure's rushing into his room, and he recalls only blackness after that.

(© 1987 Ted Jacobs, courtesy of William Morrow & Co.)

His next conscious recollection was of being in a small circular chamber under a domed ceiling, surrounded by operating tables and overwhelmed with extreme dread. He writes: "It was a truly awful sensation, accompanied by the sense that I was absolutely helpless in the hands of these strange creatures." His memories are indistinct, as if covered by amnesia, and it was under hypnosis that the entire incident was gradually unveiled. Strieber recalls the episode with such terrified emotion that it gives his incredible story all the more credibility.

He remembered being shown a needle and told that they intended to insert it into his brain. "If I had been afraid before, I now became quite crazed with terror." One of the beings asked him, "What can we do to help you stop screaming?"

Strieber's unexpected reply was, "Let me smell you."

The odor seemed to give him what he needed, "an anchor in reality. It was not a human smell, but the smell of something living," then the next thing he knows, there's a bang and a flash, and he knew that they had performed the operation on his head.

"Then the stocky ones drew my legs apart," Strieber writes. "The next thing I knew I was being shown an enormous and extremely ugly object, at least a foot long and narrow. They inserted this thing into my rectum. I had the impression that I was being raped, and for the first time I felt anger."

The alien standing before him then tapped him on the head with a wand, and "beneath the feather-pounding of the silver wand," Strieber recalls seeing pictures of our planet blowing apart, and hearing a voice saying, "That is your home. You know why this will happen." Strieber believes that he was shown images of the future of the world.

Whitley Strieber

The following morning, Strieber awoke with a sense of unease. His wife reports that his personality deteriorated dramatically over the following weeks. Indeed, Strieber was thinking quietly and calmly to himself, "I'm going mad!" Or else he was the victim of some rare brain disorder, easily leading to hallucinations or paranoia, or perhaps some other psychosis too frightening to even entertain.

Then he recalled their smell: "It was totally real memory that saved me from going stark raving mad." And above all, he remembered how it was to be with them ,the fear, the awe, and even a love.

Odor is an excellent trigger of memory, and with it, Strieber recalled those visitors with their large black insect eyes that seemed to glare into the center of his soul. And their bald heads and big slanted eyes, which gave them a fierce look. Strieber hastens to add, "And yet, I did not have the feeling that they were hostile as much as stern. They were also at least somewhat frightened of me. I was certain of that."

Who can explain what came and spirited Strieber away

into the night, perhaps injecting something into his brain? We're talking about a man who believes that he was forcibly abducted and taken aboard a spaceship by other-worldly visitors.

For the previous three years, Strieber had been working on books about nuclear war and the collapse of our environment. He knew that the planet was headed for some trying times, but he was unprepared for this. "I did not believe in UFOs at all," he writes, "and I would have laughed in the face of anybody who claimed contact. Period. I am not a candidate for conversion to any new religion that involves belief in benevolent space brothers."

Eventually, however, Strieber had to accept the terrifying realization that something had indeed happened to him: "Perhaps it did involve visitors from somewhere—maybe even from the inside the human unconscious. But there are deep, deep waters running here. If they are indeed visitors, they know us well, better than we know ourselves."

Ultimately, though, Strieber considers it to be "an intimate intrusion into the soul."

Except perhaps for one not-so-minor detail: Strieber recalls arguing with the aliens who were about to perform the operation on him, and them reassuring him—"We won't hurt you." Strieber screamed back, "You have absolutely no right." And the beings replied, "But we do have a right. You are our chosen one."

If so, Strieber was an unwilling ambassador.

Strieber adds: "Nor did I feel that they were simply studying me. Not at all. They had changed me, done something to me. In some sense, their emergence into human consciousness seemed to me to represent life—engaged in some deep act of creation. Had communion somehow come alive within me?"

Hypnosis eventually revealed that Strieber had undergone many abductions, a lifetime pattern happening since age twelve. In the years following the release of *Communion*, many other abductees have stepped forward and undergone hypnosis, only to discover that they have all had these encounters at least a dozen times. They have also said that they believe subconsciously that they did agree to this monitoring a long time ago.

Under hypnosis, they are able to report many of the same observations about the experience, including the smallness of the beings, their large black eyes, those operating tables, and the fact that there was often more than one type of alien species present.

Many of the abductees also seem to have a relationship with a particular being, which brings up perhaps the main reason behind these abductions: The genetic manipulation of Mankind. These abductees tell of having sexual experiences with these nonhuman visitors, of the suctioning of semen, and of disappearing pregnancies, but most have trouble remembering completely what transpired on those small operating tables. As one abductee noted, you try and detach yourself from the situation, "like it's not happening to you."

Many of the women abductees claim that they were taken to meet their babies—alien-human hybrids—sired by the aliens and not their human lovers. They believe they were shown these babies to check their emotional response to the hybrid beings.

The one overall feeling shared among the abductees is that "You want them to share with your intelligence what they're doing, rather than forcing you to be a part of it," but these visitors seem to be keeping a jealous hold on their secrets.

And among abductees, communication with these visitors is almost universally associated with catastrophic predictions. These people are told of impending wars, of earthquakes, of polar shifts and the coming of new ages of ice or heat. Some are also being warned that a meteorite may be heading our way, the implication here being that an asteroid may hit the planet Earth like a giant fastball pitch.

"I think they're getting ready to start another world," writes one abductee. "Ours is ending, and they've implied that to me."

"This world is going to be a different place," writes another. "It won't necessarily be a bad place, but for those who can't adapt, survival will be difficult. It will be for the young and the strong."

Strieber himself writes that he has been shown graphic depictions of our planet simply exploding.

Either way, these abductees say that they feel as if they are being used as human specimens, continuously monitored, often with implants pushed far up into their noses, and studied for years.

Strieber devoted a section of his book to the symbol of the Trinity—the Triangle. He describes it as the most common symbolic structure of the visitors. Philosopher Buckminster Fuller called the triangle "the fundamental building block of the Universe." Strieber believes that the idea behind the triad as a creative energy is of two opposite forces coming into balance, and thus creating a third force. When all three are in harmony, they become a fourth thing—an indivisible whole.

"If visitors are really here," Strieber writes, "one could say that they are orchestrating our awareness of them very carefully. It's almost as if they arrived here for the first time in the late forties. People apparently started to be abducted by them almost immediately, although few remembered this or reported it until the mid-sixties."

Strieber points out that in the fifties, these spacecraft were seen only from a distance, then they began to be observed at closer range so that by the early sixties, there were many reports of close encounters. Although Betty and Barney Hill were the first nationally-known UFO abductees (*Look Magazine*, 1966), it wasn't until Strieber's "Grey alien" book cover hit the bookstores that others like him began discovering en masse this presence in their lives.

"Over the past forty or so years," Strieber writes, "their involvement with us has not only been deepening, it has been spreading rapidly throughout society. I would not be surprised if these visitors are real and are slowly coming into contact with us according to an agenda of their own devising, which proceeds as human understanding increases."

Strieber also makes another interesting observation: "They

were very careful to keep me under control at all times, and I think that I may know the reason for their peculiar manner of dealing with us. The source of their reticence is not contempt but fear, and a well-grounded fear, too. They are not afraid of man's savagery, or his greed, but of his capacity for independent action."

In other words, our free will scares them.

This was another common theme among other abductees. They feel these beings are afraid of us, and that the abduction experiences are just as intense and frightening for the visitors. But then the question arises: Why don't these visitors understand our individual freedom. Don't ETs have free will?

"I kept returning to the thought that they may be a sort of hive," Strieber writes. "If this were true, then they may be, in effect, a single mind with millions of bodies—a brilliant creature, but lacking the speed of independent, quick-witted Mankind. As a hive, they might be strong, and we would be no match for them, but as separate individuals, a fast-thinking human being could be a remarkable threat."

On the plus side, Strieber considers what a truly intelligent hive mind might have achieved, where members have lost their identities to become incorporated into a larger collective identity.

Strieber speculates that so little is known about this phenomenon that it's impossible to do more than speculate. The visitors could be (1) coming from other planets (2) coming from Earth, but a different dimension from us (3) coming from this dimension but a different time (time travel) (4) coming from within our own collective mass consciousness.

No matter what the answer is, Strieber has no doubts. "Something is happening. This is clear."

Then there's the little matter of the U.S. Government.

Strieber writes: "In my research, I found an undertone of claims that the Government knows more about this matter than it was saying. Real documents that seemed to be false. False documents that seem to be real. And drifting through it all, the thin smoke of an incredible story. Can it be that the

Government is somehow compelled to act as it does? Certainly the combination of the visitor and Government secrecy has lead to profound public confusion."

Unfortunately for Strieber, he cannot set it all aside and go about business as usual. "I was disappearing into the night. I remembered probes going into my brain. Now it's the experience of trying to live a normal life without knowing for certain what is real." He likens it to "a psychological razor," where one has to accept and reject at the same time.

Strieber ultimately writes, "Transformation is a matter of delivering one's self into the possession of God. It would be hard for me to think that the relationship between two intelligent species would not be dense with creative potential. Communion is as wide as all the knowledge of both partners, as deep as their whole souls. Out of communion, there emerges transformation. The strong body, the brave heart, and the intelligence of a human being."

Near the end of the book, Strieber relates a story of a Japanese General who sighted some "mysterious swinging lights in a nighttime sky." A subsequent investigation by a deciding committee finally decreed that "it was only the wind making the stars sway." The year was 1235 A.D.

Seven hundred and fifty years later, Strieber points out, in a world far different from the one our forefathers knew, when it comes to the supernatural or the paranormal, the official explanation is still "the wind making the stars sway."

For not only governments, but also religions are threatened by UFOs. The existence of an alien nation would eradicate the planet's established order of religious beliefs. Science fiction writer Arthur C. Clarke probably put it best when he wrote, "The rash assertion that 'God created man in his own image' is ticking like a timebomb at the foundation of many faiths."

"I look toward the night sky," writes Strieber, "and it draws me. I'm not only scared and upset, frankly I'm also curious. I want to know what's going on out there. As I watch, the night sky grows a little darker.

"Something is out there, and it wants in."

I attended a signing for Strieber's latest book *Confirmation: The Hard Evidence of Aliens Among Us* at a Hollywood book store. After having our picture taken together, I took a seat to listen to his forty-five minute lecture.

The "hard evidence" in question is an implant in the outer edge of Strieber's ear. Strieber claims that when the implant is activated, his ear turns red and he hears a warbling tone. He went to a doctor to have it removed, but when the

Author and Strieber

initial incision was made, the implant moved over. The doctor made a second cut, and the implant moved over again. The doctor told Strieber that he might not be able to remove the implant without taking a good portion of the ear with it, so the implant was left in place and the incisions sutured back up. The purpose of the implant is still a mystery.

As Strieber spoke, what I heard were the words of an angry and frustrated man. Aside from being harassed by aliens, Strieber feels he gets little respect from the UFO community, and absolutely no help from the U.S. Government, whom he believes is well aware of the alien situation. "I want the Government to do whatever they can to help me," he stressed, "and if they can't help me—to admit it. But a pervasive secrecy governs our society. We are governed by secrecy, not the ballot. Our Black Budget is what dictates this society. As a result, the public is being left in the dark about many things."

Strieber seemed candid as he paced before the audience. He knows what his experiences have been, and if some have branded him a kook, so be it. But think about it: "A Black Budget of billions upon billions of dollars—who knows how much—is being spent without telling the public anything about how these dollars are being spent. Without anyone knowing where all these dollars are all going. This is unacceptable. We have a secrecy-obsessed bureaucracy, and so history becomes a lie." Obviously, someone very powerful is pulling the strings of this Black Budget.

Strieber then fielded questions from the audience. My hand raised first. I decided that it would be rude to ask for a closer look at the ear implant, so instead I asked him about the state of the publishing industry regarding UFO books. They seldom seem heavily advertised. Is there a UFO market today?

> "Agents and publishers will go where the dollars are," replied Strieber, "but it's the public who show lack of interest. There is still a vast public denial of extraterrestrial activity going on around them."

What happened to the twenty million readers who bought your first book? Did they buy it just for the novelty?

> "Exactly. They bought it and read it as fiction because the story's possibility was too fantastic to be true. Through the medium of fiction, however, especially in films and TV, I think that the public is beginning to become comfortable with the idea of alien interaction."

The title of your book *Breakthrough*, as opposed to *Breakdown*, says a lot. How did you mentally survive your first traumatizing abduction experiences?

> "Budd Hopkins, without whom I would have committed suicide. I hung onto his books. He was the only one who understood any of what I was saying." [Hopkins wrote *Missing Time* (Marek, 1981), the first book to bring the alien abduction phenomenon to national attention.]

The beginning quote in your novel *Majestic* (the supposedly true story behind the Roswell crash of 1947) reads: "Through official secrecy and ridicule, many citizens are led to believe that unidentified flying objects are nonsense. To hide the facts, the Air Force has silenced its personnel." This is Admiral Roscoe Hillenkoetter, First Director of the CIA, as quoted by the *New York Times* (Feb. 28, 1960). How did you come by your Roswell information, such as the live captured alien, and the alleged human body parts found on the spacecraft?

> "My novel was based upon stories told to me by my uncle, Colonel Edward Strieber, and his friend General Arthur Exon, both of whom worked on the Roswell crash. My uncle was an Intelligence Officer, and after my book *Communion* came out, he said to me, 'Your book is much closer to reality than you realize.' So I put their stories together into a fiction form because I don't know what is true history."

I seldom read horror books because they never scare me. But when I finished reading *Communion*, I had an uneasy feeling when I turned out the light to go to sleep. I dreaded seeing those Greys peeking through my window, even though there is absolutely nothing to suggest I've ever been abducted by one. And I've since read of many UFOlogists who claim to have experienced the same uneasy feeling upon reading Strieber's book.

There is still the possibility, however, that being abducted is a good thing. It might mean that you *are* one of the chosen, among those to be raptured up just before the battle of Armageddon, to be set back down somewhere to help jump-start the human race.

And there must be many "chosen" ones, for back when Strieber wrote his book, he described the "visitor" to an portrait artist and put the subsequent drawing on the book's cover. The book went on to become one of the biggest selling books of the '80s, with many buyers picking up the book and saying, "I recognize that alien!" Within a short span of time, millions of

Americans simultaneously became aware of an alien presence in their midst. What a way for the visitors to announce themselves. If true, then Strieber was the unwitting host for making the introductions between these denizens of deep space and the citizens of planet Earth.

Either way, his story does serve up a spine-chilling view of a world far less certain than we could suspect. His book scared me when I turned off the light at night. It made me want to close my eyes tight as I drifted off to sleep and "into the great uncertainty." And I'm sure that dreams are just the tip of the iceberg.

So is this alien abduction phenomenon nuts-and-bolts, or just nuts? Until we see a shred of evidence on the matter, we'll have to be content with the frightened pleasures of our imaginations.

When I finished writing this review, I took another glance at the "visitor" on the book's cover before turning the book face down. That Grey alien still gives me the creeps.

Maybe I *am* an abductee.

Communion: A True Story
(Avon, 1987)
      Whitley Strieber

For information on The Communtion
Foundation, a nonprofit research group
into the close encounter phenomenon,
write to:
      Whitley Strieber
      5928 Broadway, #263
      San Antonio, Texas 78209

      www.strieber.com

Chapter Eleven

The Sudden Sumerian

From the barren wastes

of a Near Eastern desert

Without forewarning –

sprang civilization

Now a scholar's translation of

their clay tablets puts

A whole new slant on Adam and Eve

in the Garden of Eden

The Sudden Sumerian

The Book of Genesis is the first book in what is commonly referred to as the Old Testament. In Hebrew, it's known as *Bereshith*, after its opening phrase "In The Beginning." Scholars believe that it was originally written sometime around 2500 B.C., and while its authorship has been attributed to Moses, recent discoveries have revealed that the biblical creation tales are merely a summary version of more ancient traditions.

The first chapter of Genesis tells the cosmology of the Universe, spending a scant twenty-five verses on its creation of light from darkness, firmament from a void. Then we read that on the sixth day of creation, "God said, Let *us* make man in *our* image, after *our* likeness" (Gen. 1:26). Theologians and scholars have been puzzling and arguing over who "us" is ever since. For in what an image they made us: two arms, two legs, and a head, not to mention a whole range of emotions, such as love and hate, hope and fear, pride and despair.

But it's the use of the plural pronoun, in three separate instances, that stumps the scholars. The Book of Genesis has a plurality problem. It's a problem of biblical proportions, and no one has been able to provide a satisfactory answer.

That is, until Zecharia Sitchin, a Hebrew scholar, and one of the few scholars of antiquity to be able to read Sumerian, was able to piece together prior translations of millennia-old Sumerian clay tablets. These baked-clay tablets, discovered in the ruins of ancient Mesopotamia, form the oldest narrative literature in the world, a written legacy from Mankind's most ancient civilization.

Sitchin acknowledges the legion of scholars before him, uncovering and deciphering these cuneiform writings, that allowed him to come up with the true meaning behind the biblical tales. He found that when he stood the Sumerian clay tablets and the Hebrew Genesis side by side, it shed new light on the stories of the Garden of Eden, the Great Flood of Noah, and the Tower of Babel.

Sitchin's startling revelation answers the big question: How did civilization come about? Scientists agree that by all accounts Mankind should still be without civilization. And yet, seemingly overnight, the first civilization, known as Sumer (circa 3800 B.C.), flowered up suddenly from the barren wastes of a Near Eastern desert. The human species unexpectedly became civilized, planting crops and making pottery. It's as if a mysterious hand had raised Mankind up to a level of culture and knowledge.

THE ASTOUNDING, OVERWHELMINGLY DOCUMENTED STORY OF EARTH'S CELESTIAL ANCESTORS.

BOOK I OF THE EARTH CHRONICLES

BY THE AUTHOR OF THE STAIRWAY TO HEAVEN AND THE WARS OF GODS AND MEN

"The book should be as talked about as von Däniken." *Library Journal*

THE 12th PLANET

by ZECHARIA SITCHIN

(Courtesy of Avon Books)

"The Sumerians, the people through whom this high civilization so suddenly came into being," writes Sitchin in his book *The 12th Planet*, "had a ready answer: Whatever seems beautiful, we made by the grace of the gods."

Who were these gods of Sumer?

Genesis refers to them as *Nefilim* ("Those Who Came Down"). These were the same gods described by Greek mythology, said to be living on Earth long before Mankind had been created. Known as the race of Titans, they were powerful beings, capable of heroic feats beyond mortal comprehension. They were able to ascend into the heavens and roam the skies at will. The Milky Way was said to be the starry road to their heavenly abode. Yet these gods not only looked like humans, but displayed virtually every human emotion, such as love and hate, hope and fear, pride and despair.

Each god had a distinct personality, and their battles among themselves for divine succession led to the Wars of the Gods. But the Sumerian clay tablets leave no doubt that these gods were indeed living beings, flesh and blood creatures who literally came down to Earth from the heavens. And that they had arrived in some kind of flying machine.

Sitchin writes that the pictographic sign for 'gods' in Sumerian is a two-syllable word: DIN.GIR. DIN means "righteous" or "just." The meaning for GIR is a rocket. Put together, it translates as "divine beings," or, more explicitly, "the just ones of the blazing rockets."

"Irrespective of the theological implications," writes Sitchin, "the literal and original meaning of the Genesis verses cannot be escaped: The "sons of the gods" who came to Earth from the heavens were the Nefilim. And they were the People of the Rocketships."

Speculation that Earth has been visited by intelligence from elsewhere leads one to investigate the other planets of our Solar System. Sitchin found that the writings of the ancient Near East speak clearly of a planet from which these gods had come. And their description of the frequent travel of the gods between Earth and their Heavenly Abode would place this "heaven" within our own Solar System, and not some distant galaxy.

The Sumerians claim that our Solar System is a "family" of twelve members: the Sun and Moon and ten—not nine—planets. They say that this extra planet is named NIBIRU ("Planet of the Crossing"). And that this planet is the home of the Nefilim.

And in a surprising revelation, the Sumerians even named the sun APSU ("One Who Exists from the Beginning") as the center of our Solar System, millennia before Western man confirmed this belief. How can it be that these Sumerians knew all this? "Not because they had better instruments than we do," writes Sitchin, "but because their source of information was the Nefilim."

These clay tablets tell a story about gods who arrived upon the Earth, not for a quick exploratory visit, but to establish a permanent "home away from home." (Sitchin estimates that they first landed on earth some 450,000 years ago.) The planet was in the midst of its Ice Age, with about a third of Earth covered with ice sheets and glaciers.

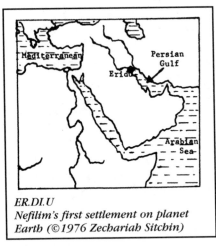

ER.DI.U
Nefilim's first settlement on planet
Earth (©1976 Zechariah Sitchin)

According to these fragmentary texts, the Nefilim apparently splashed down in the Persian Gulf, with one of their first concerns having to do with watery marshes. The name of their leader has been forever recorded; E.A was his name. And we know that they named their first settlement E.RI.DU ("house in faraway built")." To this day, the Persian term *ordu* means encampment, or settlement. But why would they arrive to establish a lonely outpost on a half-frozen planet?

In his book *Genesis Revisited* (Avon Books, 1990), the companion volume to his *The Earth Chronicles* series of books, Sitchin concludes that they might have come to earth for gold, a metal we've come to think of as the royal metal. Sumerian pictographs reveal a great familiarity with the mining of metals going on at the time, and there is still much evidence of prehistoric mining in South Africa, even today a major source of the world's mined gold.

"On their planet Nibiru," writes Sitchin, "the Nefilim might have been facing a situation we on Earth may also soon face: ecological deterioration was making life increasingly impossible. There was a need to protect their dwindling atmosphere, and the only solution seemed to be to suspend gold particles above it, as a shield. (Windows on American spacecraft, for example, are coated with a thin layer of gold to shield the astronauts from radiation.)"

But somebody had to work these mines, and according to the Sumerian texts, those who did the manual labor were the lesser members of the landing party. They had the unpleasant task of going into the depths of the African soil and doing the actual mining. Soon, however, these Nefilim tired of the toil, and the tablets say they cried, "No more!" And they mutinied.

The tale goes on to say that the Supreme Ruler sided with the workers, and descended from his Heavenly Abode to planet Earth to mediate. Then one of the gods had a solution: Let's create a *lulu* ("Primitive Worker") who can bear the yoke and take over the burden of work. The Sumerian term for "Man" is *LU*, but its root word conveys the notion of mixing.

Sitchin writes: "In the Sumerian versions, the decision to create Man was adopted by the gods in their Assembly." Significantly, the Book of Genesis also uses the plural *Elohim* (literally, "deities") to denote "God," and reports an astonishing remark: "And Elohim said, Let us make Man in our image, after our likeness." The Old Testament made it clear that Man was not a god but created of the *adamah*, the Earth's soil. Genesis refers to this creature as "the Adam," not a person, but literally "the Earthling."

The creation of Mankind has always been the center of controversy between science and religion. Science teaches that Mankind is the result of evolution, which may explain how life on Earth evolved, but it does not explain how life on Earth began. Creationists, on the other hand, believe in the Judeo-

Christian doctrine of *creatio ex nihilo*, or "creation out of nothing." But while they assert Man's instantaneous creation, they have a hard time reconciling Mankind's close similarity to the monkey.

"There is really no conflict at all between the two," writes Sitchin. "The Sumerians described Man as both a deliberate creature of the gods and a link in the evolutionary chain. While the apelike *Homo erectus* was a product of evolution, *Homo sapiens*—modern Man—was a new creature brought about by the ancient gods. Here, then, is the answer to the puzzle: The Nefilim did not 'create' Man out of nothing; rather, they took an existing creature and manipulated it, to 'bind upon it' the 'image of the gods.'"

And the human race does share much in common with the animal kingdom, such as the blood type Rh positive, which refers to the rhesus monkey, and the curious fact that human embryos have a rudimentary tail. Genetically speaking, humankind is closest to the chimpanzee. All of this suggests that at some time, Mankind underwent some substantial DNA splicing.

Sitchin suggests that the process used to achieve this quick evolutionary advancement of *Homo erectus* was genetic manipulation, the "imprinting" of the image of the gods onto the being that already existed. Assuming that the Nefilim were capable of space travel 450,000 years ago, would they not also be equally advanced in other sciences as well?

The Old Testament offers only meager clues on how this creation took place: "And the Lord God formed man of the dust of the ground, and breathed into his nostrils the breath of life; and man became a living soul" (Gen. 2:7).

The Sumerian clay tablets, however, are quite explicit on the subject. They say it involved the use of the male genes of a god, as the divine element, and the female genes of a *Homo erectus*, as the earthly element, fertilizing the ovum of an ape-woman with the sperm of a god.

"The tablets state that the Nefilim's blood was mixed into the clay," writes Sitchin, "so as to bind god and man genetically

*Note the goddess holds a newborn child, flanked by the
Tree of Life and laboratory flasks (©1976 Zechariah Sitchin)*

to the end of days." He notes that the Sumerian word for clay is
TI.IT ("that which is with life"). "Clay, we discover, has two
basic properties essential to life: the capacity to store and the
ability to transfer energy. It might have acted as a chemical lab."

As for breathing in the "spirit of life," the tablets say that the
place where this procedure took place was SHI.IM.TI ("the
house where the wind of life is breathed in"). This is virtually
identical to the biblical statement of "blew in his nostrils the
breath of life" in how the first Earthling was brought forth.

It is here that we must take note of the numerous Sumerian
references to the much "mixing of two life-sources" together.
This corresponds with the chimeras of Greek mythology,
which includes such creatures as the Centaur (half man, half
horse), and the Satyr (goat-man). Figures of cat-women and
men with birds' heads adorn many of the Egyptian and Assyrian
bas-reliefs found in the Near East ruins. Perhaps these mon-
strosities of antiquity were not just figments of an artist's
imagination, but the trial-and-error experiments that came out
of the laboratories of the Nefilim.

According to the Book of Genesis, the Deity brought the
newly-created Earthling "eastward" and "put him in the garden
of Eden to tend it and keep it" (Gen. 2:15). The Sumerian name
for the gods' abode was E.DIN ("home of the righteous one"),

described as a place of temperate climate. Genesis relates that it was watered by four major rivers, two of which, the Tigris and the Euphrates, are present today, placing this fabled garden somewhere near modern-day Iraq.

Genesis describes how the Earthling tended the orchard all alone, and the Deity took pity on his loneliness. So the Earthling was put into a deep sleep, and a rib was removed. Sitchin points out that the Elohim now used a piece of bone to construct a woman, demonstrating the power of DNA.

DNA, a chemical compound made up of four nucleotides, forms the genetic blueprint of every living thing on earth. Indeed, scientists say that genetic evidence suggests that the entire human species could have descended from a single female ancestor.

The biblical tale of Adam and Eve in the Garden of Eden opens with the statement: "And the both of them were naked, the man and his mate, and they were not ashamed" (Gen 2:25).

They tended the garden, but these Earthlings were prohibited from tasting of the fruit of the Tree of Knowing that grew in the middle of the orchard. However, even under the prohibition of death, human nature being what it is (Nefilim nature?), the Earthlings were persuaded to go ahead and have a taste of what would make them "knowing" as the Deity.

The Deity had threatened them with death if they disobeyed (Gen. 3:3), but all that happened to them was a sudden awareness that they were naked, for no sooner had they acquired this "knowing" than "the eyes of them both were open." They sewed some fig leaves together and made themselves aprons, but true to the Serpent's word, the man and woman did not die.

When the Deity found out, he put a curse on the Serpent, and in a surprise move, he made the Earthlings "coats of skins, and clothed them." It's here that the Genesis Deity again lapses into the plural: "Behold, the man has become one of *us*, to know good and evil" (Gen. 3:22).

"Throughout the Old Testament," writes Sitchin, "the term 'to know' is used to denote sexual intercourse for the purpose of procreation. Was the purpose of the story of the temptation in the Garden merely a dramatic way to explain how Man came to wear clothes? Or was the wearing of clothes merely an outward manifestation of the new 'knowing?'"

Either way, the Earthlings could now produce children on their own. And Sitchin notes that it was only after Man's acquisition of this "knowing" that Genesis ceases to refer to him as "the Adam" and calls him by the proper name Adam. It is also here that Adam first calls his wife Eve ("She of Life"), for she would become "the mother of all who live."

For their sin of disobedience, the Deity drove them from the Garden, where they were cursed to toil and sweat in order to survive. According to *The Forgotten Books of Eden* (World Publishing, 1951), the frightened man and his mate spent the night in a cave before returning the next day to the Garden. But Gen. 3:24 says the Deity had placed "a flaming sword which turned every way" at the entrance to block their access.

Adam and Eve eventually raised a family "east of Eden." Beginning with Cain and Abel, it was a lineage that lasted for ten generations, until Noah, the hero of the Deluge.

"I will destroy man whom I have created off the face of the Earth" (Gen. 6:7).

What could have upset the Deity so terribly that he decided to send a deluge of water to wash away Mankind? Sitchin points out that the repeated use of the term "flesh" could be a clue. "The sons of Elohim saw that the daughters of men were fair, and they took themselves wives of all which they chose" (Gen 6:2). Had Man had become a sex maniac? No, it was the gods themselves. Apparently, the Nefilim had become so completely enamored with the new creature's females that they couldn't keep their hands off them.

The idea of male gods coupling with mortal women whose beauty flames their desire is commonplace in Greek myth. And in all creation stories, this intermingling of human and divine is not approved of and seen as crossing the line. The offspring of this coupling between gods and women was seen as defiling the lineage, and thus the Assembly of the Gods ordained the Flood.

Geological evidence shows that a flood once did cover a major portion of the earth. Scientists theorize that this could have been the aftermath of the planet's last Ice Age, which came to an abrupt end about 13,000 years ago. According to the Sumerian tablets, when "the Flood streamed over the Earth," the Nefilim took to their shuttlecraft, and the gods fled the Earth.

The Sumerian Deluge texts tell us that it was the god E.A who, in defiance of the Assembly, forewarned Mankind and aided him in escaping the disaster. Greek mythology names this champion as Prometheus.

In Genesis, the man who heard the warning was Noah ("righteous man"). In the Sumerian account, his name was Ziusudra ("exceedingly wise"). Greek mythology names him as Deucalion.

For forty days and nights, the Earth was inundated by water. Sitchin believes a series of tidal waves, caused by the melting of the polar ice caps, washed over the planet. Yet somehow, Mankind survived.

But if the Deluge was a traumatic experience for *Homo sapiens*, it devastated the gods. The planet Earth lay buried under mud. The Deity immediately felt remorse, and he blessed the survivors, permitting them to "be fruitful and multiply." In Greek mythology, he sends Iris, the goddess of the rainbow, across the skies in promise to never flood the earth again. The Deity in the Book of Genesis does the same.

The gods returned to Earth and lost no time in imparting gifts to Mankind. Genesis confirms that the first cultivated food after the Deluge was the grape, which Noah drank of its wine in excess. The relationship between the gods and the Earthlings had changed, as they decided to give the human species civilization.

This first post-flood civilization, Sumer, appearing out of nowhere some 6,000 years ago, is credited with virtually all the "firsts" of Earthly human advancement.

The list includes the first written language, Sumerian, whose wedge-shaped writing known as cuneiform, is the original script from which all other writing is derived. More than any other invention, writing made civilization possible.

Records show that it was in Sumer that the first known wheeled vehicles were used. Scholars consider the Sumerian solid wooden wheel as the greatest mechanical invention of all time.

Sumeria also possessed an amazingly vast knowledge of astronomy, which led to their establishment of the first calendar.

Another major Sumerian achievement was agriculture. Many scholars believe that ancient Sumeria became a civilization largely because of its ingenuity in building dams and canals, which allowed them to divert the Tigris and Euphrates Rivers to water the barren desert for farming. Mesopotamia—"The Land between Rivers"—was a veritable food basket in ancient times.

And from where did the seeds for these grains come?

"The seeds, the Sumerians say," writes Sitchin, "were a gift sent to Earth by the

Note the rocketship in the skies (©1976 Zechariah Sitchin)

Deity from his Celestial Abode. Wheat, barley and hemp were lowered to Earth from the Twelfth Planet." According to Greek mythology, the greatest gift of all came from Prometheus, who brought Mankind fire. In the fourth millennium B.C., the gods made Sumer "the cradle of civilization."

This relationship between the gods and Mankind, however, apparently turned soured, for we now have the third and final episode of the use of the plural pronoun in the book of Genesis: "Come, let *us* go down and confound their language, that they many not understand one another's speech" (Gen. 11:7).

It is the well-known biblical story of the Tower of Babel, where the Deity got worried because Mankind was building a tower to "reach unto heaven." The Sumerian tablets say that the "tower" was actually some sort of a spacecraft launching pad. Both accounts agree that it angered the Deity, and that he deliberately caused a confusion of Man's tongue. The human species, which had been speaking one language, was suddenly speaking in a multitude of tongues, and it sounded like babbling.

Sitchin notes that the word "babel" comes from *Bab-ili*, meaning "gateway of the gods." He suggests the moral was: "The flying machines were meant for the gods and not for Mankind."

The eventual destiny of Sumeria turned out to be the fate of all earthly kingdoms when around the 24th century B.C., King Sargon led the Akkadian nation and conquered the city-states of Sumer, absorbing them into what would become the world's first major empire. Sargon, history's first legendary ruler, was said to be born of a lowly mother, set adrift in "an ark of bulrushes" on the waters of the Euphrates, and rescued by a gardener, eventually rising to become leader and king. This mythological background became the model for a whole lineage of heroes from the Greek Perseus to the Hebrew Moses.

So where exactly did these Nefilim come from?

Sitchin writes that the tablets known as the "Epic of Creation" state clearly that the formation of our planet was a cataclysmic event referred to as the Celestial Battle: "Into our original Solar System (I estimate the time about four billion years ago), an Invader appeared. The Sumerians called it NIBIRU."

It came with its own satellites (moons), entering our Solar System "as if approaching combat." It was on its elliptical orbit around the sun. "According to Sumerian evidence," writes Sitchin, "Nibiru orbits the sun like a comet, with the Sun at extreme focus, so that the distance from the Sun would be almost the whole major axis, not just half of it."

Its approach stirred up electrical and other atmospheric conditions from the other members of the solar system. Its gravitational forces pushed aside the smaller celestial bodies, but it was headed on a collision course with planet TI.AMAT ("Maiden of Life"). The two gigantic planets did not collide, however. It was several of Nibiru's moons that smashed into Tiamat, which was caught up in the magnetic and gravitational pull of Nibiru and was unable to slip away.

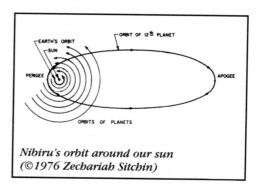

Nibiru's orbit around our sun (©1976 Zechariah Sitchin)

According to the Epic of Creation, the impact with the large moons broke the planet Tiamat in two, the upper half eventually rounding out (through gravitational forces) to become the planet Earth as we know it. Nibiru then smashed into the lower half of Tiamat on its return orbit from around the sun, shattering it and stretching the pieces into a great celestial band, "hammered together to become a bracelet" in the heavens. Today, this great band is known as the Asteroid Belt.

This twelfth member of our Solar System then continued on its vast elliptical orbit around the sun. Meanwhile, the new planet, Earth, settled into its celestial orbit around the Sun (giving us our seasons), slowly turning on its axial spin (giving us day and night).

Sitchin writes: "In perfect accord, both the Book of Genesis and the Epic of Creation state that this was the beginning of life upon earth." For this celestial collision also "seeded" the new planet with its life, "living creatures that swarm and fowls that fly." "Seeded from space" is what Sitchin says are the very words written down millennia ago by the Sumerians.

The Sumerian tablets indicate that the grand orbit of Nibiru returns it to Earth's vicinity about every 3600 years. Sitchin believes that this coincides with the crucial phases of Man's development, which can be placed at intervals of about 3600 years. It is not unlikely, then, that these Nefilim have been instrumental in Mankind's progression, passing on knowledge each time their planet returns to Earth.

This twelfth planet would also give astrologers twelve celestial bodies, and not just eleven, for the twelve houses of the zodiac.

How could the Sumerians have known all of this cosmology and astronomy so long ago, at the dawn of civilization? The Sumerian tablets say that the Nefilim told them. And the Twelfth Planet is the home of the Nefilim.

And astonishing as it may sound, astronomers have been looking for a missing planet in our solar system. "For some time," writes Sitchin, "astronomers who have been puzzled by perturbations in the orbits of Uranus and Neptune considered the possibility of the existence of one more planet farther out from the Sun. They designate it Planet X, meaning both 'unknown' and 'tenth.'"

Sitchin postulates that Planet X and Nibiru will be one and the same.

I spoke to Sitchin in New York by phone. He speaks with a heavy accent, and he chooses his words carefully. He preferred to answer my questions on paper. My first question brought up the fact that he is one of the few scholars able to read and understand Sumerian. Please tell us something of this world that you are able to see into.

"I see a civilization that blossomed out suddenly and as if

Zecharia Sitchin (Courtesy of Zecharia Sitchin)

out of nowhere some 6,000 years ago," replied Sitchin, "and within a very short time gave rise to virtually all the 'firsts' of what one deems essential to a high civilization to this day.

"The Sumerians were truly the first 'people of the book.' They wrote everything down: temple sacrifices, names of daily laborers and their rations, marriage contracts (and divorces); and on the other hand, songs, temple hymns, and the source of all their knowledge: Tales of the 'gods', the ANUNNAKI, 'Those Who From Heaven To Earth Came.' The Bible called them Nefilim, meaning 'Those Who Have Come Down.'"

Who were these Nefilim?

"That question, asked by me at Hebrew school, launched me into the search led me to the Sumerians and the Anunnaki. A great number of texts written on clay tablets (only a fraction of what had been has been found by archaeologists; only a fraction of what has been found has been transcribed and translated) deal with the affairs, identities and origins of the Anunnaki/Nefilim. The other scholars call them 'myths.' I say: What IF? What if what the ancients knew and recorded had really happened?"

This would coincide with Plato, who wrote: "We must accept the tradition of the men of old time who affirm themselves to be the offspring of the gods, and surely they must have known their own ancestors. We are of the heavenly race of gods."

"I believe they used genetic engineering to 'create' the Adam—*Homo sapiens*—by upgrading the hominoids who had evolved on Earth."

Tell us about their planet Nibiru.

"The 'myths' relate how a planet thrust out
of its original solar system passed by ours,
collided with another existing planet in our
solar system, and shifted part of the broken
up planet to a new orbit to become planet
Earth. The invader itself was then caught in a
permanent solar orbit. The Sumerians called
it Nibiru, meaning Planet of the Crossing (its
earliest symbol was a cross!) That planet
periodically returns to our vicinity, passing
between Mars and Jupiter. It has been at
such times, the Sumerians (and the Old
Testament) assert, that the Anunnaki/Nefilim
started to come and go between their planet
and Earth."

Is there a possibility of this Twelfth Planet returning in time
to save Earth from its seemingly downward spiral?

"From the earliest times, the periodic return
of Nibiru to our vicinity has been recalled by
Mankind as a time of change—sometimes for
the better (more knowledge, advancement,
prosperity); sometimes as the cause of catastrophic events, such as the Deluge. All
civilizations and cultures, in the Old World
and in the New World, have similar tales, similar recollections, and similar expectations of
The Return. There can be no doubt that the
present-day expectations that a change is
coming are related to the ancient records
and beliefs."

And what do you think will happen when Nibiru returns?

"Will it usher in a messianic era? Will it cause
untold havoc and calamities? Will Mankind
survive? Will Mankind be better after that?
The answers take one from the realm of
ancient records and knowledge of the past

to speculation about the future, and speculation is not my field."

Could these UFO sightings/alien abductions supposedly
taking place around the globe be the Nefilim beginning their
latest genetic manipulations?

"The prophecies, not least by the Bible itself,
speak of the Day of the Lord as a certainty,
not a possibility. In my book *Genesis
Revisited*, I included data from our recent
times suggesting that Mars, which did serve
as a way station for the Anunnaki/Nefilim,
has again someone present on it. If that base
has been reactivated, as much evidence suggests, it could well explain the current UFO
phenomenon. It could even explain the origin of the 'little grey people,' for as I show in
my books, the Anunnaki employed as emissaries androids, who looked very much like
the 'little grey people' that some have been
reporting in connection with UFO sightings."

Reading your books, I felt as if I were reading the works of
a man raised in the traditional Hebrew "One God" belief, who
now interprets that "One God" to have taken a step back, with
a race of "gods" now as our direct Creator(s). Do you still
believe in a One God as the Creator of all?

"Yes, I do believe in God with a capital G, the
Creator of the whole Universe and everything in it. But I also believe that this Creator
works through chosen emissaries, and in
ancient times they included the Anunnaki of
whom the Sumerians wrote. The fact that
people considered those visitors to Earth as
'gods' (with a small 'g') only increases my
belief in God with a capital G."

Reviewing Sitchin's version of the tale of Genesis, I kept
returning to his theory about how the Tower of Babel was actu-

ally a spaceship launching pad. Were these gods really worried about Mankind reaching for the stars? And if so, what about America's space program today? Or maybe these gods simply felt they were being mocked. The human race was not turning out as expected, and the "division of tongues" was meant to slow down our advancement by a couple of thousand years, until their planet returns again.

And judging by the information on those clay tablets, the Twelfth Planet is due back sometime soon. What will happen when these Nefilim return? When their planet comes around again, will they make another genetic manipulation?

Could any of this be at all possible?

Exhibit #1: Man himself. Here we are, existing on a planet, for all intents and purposes, standing as naked apes, just an evolutionary arm's length away from the chimpanzee. And yet, while the chimp has remained in the trees, we've seen Mankind soar off the face of Earth and land on the moon.

To reinterpret the Book of Genesis against the grain of all traditional religious beliefs takes, well—nerve. To propose a cosmic explanation for "Let *us* create man in *our* image" takes more than chutzpah. It takes an open mind, and Sitchin has led us into a realm of history where Mankind has forgotten to look—namely, the past, mythology, where every tale holds a kernel of truth. When we suppose that these mythological gods could be our cosmic ancestors, the past truly does comes alive.

Perhaps, then, Mankind is not the total story of creation. Perhaps we are only the middle few pages in a far longer story. That still leaves the question: If the Nefilim created Mankind, who created the Nefilim?

The only real clue we have are those four opening words of the Book of Genesis: "In the beginning God."

*The 12th Planet: Book One of The
Earth Chronicles* series (Avon, 1976)
Zecharia Sitchin

Genesis Revisited (Avon, 1990)
Zechariah Sitchin

For a listing of books and tapes, write to:
Zecharia Sitchin
P.O. Box 577
New York, New York 10185

Chapter Twelve

The Antichrist

You've heard all about him –

he's much anticipated

with his Mark of the Beast

Some say he'll be a computer

others say a clone

Either way – prophets say

he's the Apocalypse

and he's on the horizon

The Antichrist

The End Times. A scenario closely mapped out by that ancient book of prophecy—the Bible—a book once understood by only mystics and scholars until Hal Lindsey came along and laid it out into the words of *The Late Great Planet Earth*. The biggest selling nonfiction book of the '70s, it's sold over twenty-eight million copies worldwide, making it the second best selling religious book of all time, exceeded only by the Bible.

Today, as we watch much of what Lindsey wrote about taking place in the headlines, he takes no credit for having prophesied the events unfolding. He takes only credit for putting it into words that people can understand.

Lindsey's book focuses on the Book of Revelation, the last book of the New Testament, written around 70 A.D. by an old hermit known as St. John the Divine. John was living in a cave at the time, banished to the penal island of Patmos for his religious beliefs. He had been an apostle of Jesus of Nazareth, and the only one of the four Gospel writers who was an eyewitness to the crucifixion. The term Christianity had not yet been coined, but John was steadfast as he "bare record of the testimony of Jesus Christ, and of all things that he saw."

John wrote that one day he heard a trumpet sound and

then a voice say "I am the Alpha and the Omega [the First and the Last], and what thou sees, write down into a book." It was the beginning of a nightmarish vision where John saw the End of the World (a destroying of the old and a beginning of the new). His vision has come down through the ages to be known as the Apocalypse.

Scholars have since tried to decipher the meaning of John's vision, and yet the question still remains: Is this book really a crystal ball into the unfolding events of things to come, or just the written account of one man's hallucination?

(Courtesy of Zondervan Publishing House)

According to Lindsey, the Book of Revelation is a book of prophecy telling us that we are now in the "era of the Antichrist." Every day is moving us closer to the New World Order, and the war which will bring Mankind to the brink of destruction, all of which leads up to the coming of the Messiah.

Mankind has always had the desire to know what lies ahead. Indeed, even today people are guided by horoscopes and psychic hotlines. The future is big business. Lindsey writes: "I believe this generation is overlooking the most authentic voice of all, the voice of the Hebrew prophets. The central theme of Jewish prophets is that 'the Messiah' would come and bring universal peace, prosperity, and harmony among all peoples of the Earth. The Jewish nation is the most important sign to this generation. The center of the entire forecast is Israel."

According to Lindsey, three important conditions must be met before the End Time period can begin:

First, the restoration of the state of Israel. Israel as a nation had been destroyed twice before, once by Babylon in 400 B.C., then by Rome in 70 A.D. Then in May of 1948, after almost two thousand years, Israel again became a nation, "never to be scattered again."

Second, the repossession of the city of Jerusalem by the state of Israel. In June of 1967, as a result of the six-day Arab-Israeli war, Israel took possession of Jerusalem.

The third prophecy, and presently the stumbling block to all three conditions being fulfilled: The rebuilding of the Temple of Solomon by the state of Israel. The temple itself was destroyed twice before, first by the Babylonians, then again by the Romans. Today, the only remnant of this ancient temple is the Wailing Wall, located on the west side of the Temple Mount.

Hal Lindsey

Lindsey believes this last prophecy to be of the utmost importance, for of the 613 commandments given in the Jewish Torah, one-half of them depend upon the temple being active, and the Torah tells us that the Messiah will not come until there is a full reinstatement of the Jewish worship, including animal sacrifices according to the Law of Moses. This condition demands that this temple must rebuilt because these sacrifices can only be offered in the Temple of Solomon.

Of course, Israel could reconstruct this temple anywhere, but they would prefer to rebuild it on the old temple site: Mount Moriah. There is, however, one major obstacle barring its construction there: The Dome of the Rock. This mosque, Islam's third holiest shrine, is built squarely in the middle of the

Temple Mount. The prophet Muhammad is believed to have ascended to heaven from a rock on this site. To rebuild their temple on the original site, Israel will have to replace the mosque.

But as Lindsey writes, "Obstacle or no obstacle, it is certain that the Temple will be rebuilt. Prophecy demands it." This final condition will then prepare us for the greatest moment in the world's history—the coming of the Messiah.

The problem runs deeper than the Temple Mount, however. "When the Jews reestablished their nation in Palestine," writes Lindsey, "they created an unsolvable problem: they displaced Arabs who had dwelt in Palestine for several centuries. The Jews will never be convinced that they should leave the land that God gave to their forefathers, and the Arabs are equally implacable in their unwillingness to accept the Israeli occupation of what they consider to be their land." Today, the city of Jerusalem, the Royal City, is "a cup of trembling" and a place of constant tension.

Lindsey interprets Biblical prophecy as stating that this Middle East crisis will escalate until it threatens the peace of the whole world. Then an incredible "Roman leader" will rise up to solve the dilemma in an ingenious way. He will make "a strong covenant" with the Israelis, guaranteeing their safety and protection. And somehow he'll assist them in rebuilding their temple and reinstate their worship and sacrifices.

Lindsey believes that this Roman leader will be a world politician who arises out of the still-forming European Union (EU), an effort toward a United States of Europe. It will be a revived "Roman Empire," so to speak, because the original treaty was signed in Rome (1957). The aim of the EU is for there to be one currency, and then one European army. It would be the single largest financial bloc, and military force, in the world.

"Heading this powerful revived Roman Empire," writes Lindsey, "will be a man of such magnetism and such influence that he will for a time be the greatest dictator the world has ever known. He will turn out to be the completely godless, diabolically evil creature that the Book of Revelation calls 'the Antichrist.'"

His dominance will be a reign of terror, and he will attempt to strip all individuals of their human qualities. It will be the beginning of the New World Order and a one-world Government.

The only physical clue that we have on who this leader will be is that he receives a seemingly fatal head wound, and then miraculously recovers (Rev. 13:3). The whole world will be astonished. Lindsey believes that this man will be swept into power at a time when people are so tired of war that they will give their allegiance to any politician who can deliver peace. "According to the book of Daniel," Lindsey writes, "the minute the Israeli leader and the Roman leader sign this pact, a seven-year countdown begins, noted as the Tribulation."

We do have a second clue on who this leader might be. We have his number: 666 (Rev. 13:18). It's "the Mark of the Beast." Incidentally, the numerical code for the World Wide Web—WWW—is 666. (In computer software, the numerical equivalent of the letter W is six.)

Also coincidentally, there is a three-story building in Brussels, Belgium, that houses a gigantic European Community world banking computer, known as The B.E.A.S.T. (Belgium Electronic Account Surveillance Team). The idea is to develop the EU into a cashless society, where every citizen carries a single card for all their multiple daily transactions. "Smart Cards" they're calling them.

And how is it expected that this single supercomputer will be capable of processing and storing all of this information for the entire EU? And make it available for immediate use over a vast Internet? It has something to do with "molecular construction and the precise placement of each atom."

They call it Quantum Mechanics. A quantum computer uses an entirely different, and deeper, method of storing information than today's binary computers, which use simple on/off bits processed through transistors. Quantum computers store information on "qubits" (quantum bits), which are not on or off but exist in multiple states at once. Qubits exhibit wavelike tendencies, enabling information to move more quickly.

If all computer systems were linked to one massive quantum technology, an all-powerful central brain, a giant computing system—the B.E.A.S.T.—it could solve in minutes what would take other computers hundreds of years to calculate. He could be a machine to solve many problems, answering many profound questions.

In 1997, IBM announced that their supercomputer Deep Blue would not play chess again "in the foreseeable future," saying their scientists wished to move on to other challenges. Deep Blue had just defeated world chess champion Garry Kasparov in an exhibition match. Some experts contend that computers have now surpassed the human mind in chess. IBM programmers estimate that Deep Blue was able to look at one billion chess positions per second.

All of this leads to the question: Just what do we know about Artificial Intelligence?

America's richest man, software magnate Bill Gates, has already spoken about computers holding conversations with humans, and being able to feel emotions. They're becoming conscious. Of course, as these machines become more self-aware, they'll want to become mobile, with arms and legs, and then these quantum-thinking machines will be soon be building themselves, without our help. And perhaps ordering us about.

And as for the Mark of the Beast, what better "mark" for a computer than a computer chip? With a microchip implanted under the skin, the individual will no longer have need for even a "smart card." He or she will be able to be scanned anywhere, any time. The microchip will link the individual to a central computer data base, giving the person's location via a satellite, enabling it to track his or her every move. The computer would have "a God's eye view" of you, so to speak, making George Orwell's "Big Brother" prophecy of *1984* all the more real and terrifying.

Rev. 13:16 says this "mark" will most likely be located in

your right hand, or in your forehead, and that you'll need it if you wish to buy or sell on the open market. This technology is already here in the form of tiny chips being implanted in pets "so we can find them." Parents are thinking of getting them for their children. (White House whispers have it that its Secret Service agents already have such implants.)

According to Revelation 13:11, a False Prophet will rise to the forefront with this Antichrist. This prophet will be a religious leader, appearing like a lamb but speaking like a dragon. He will do "signs and wonders" that will help convince the nation of Israel to sign the peace covenant with the Dictator. Some believe that this False Prophet will be the Pope. Catholic tradition has long believed that the final Pope, *Peter Romanus*, will defect (and/or be crucified upside down).

In 1917, Mary the Queen of Heaven, appeared to three peasant children at Fatima, Portugal, and gave them three secrets. They are said to be: (1) a description of Hell, symbolizing that God will punish evildoers (2) both a request and a prophecy, saying that if the world prayed, Russia will be converted, and (3) the third secret has never been revealed.

However, one of the children, Lucia, wrote them down into a letter which was given to the Pope, with instructions that it was not to be opened until 1960, when its contents could then be revealed. In 1960, Pope John XXIII supposedly opened the letter, read it (some say he fainted), then refused to say what the third prophecy was. Speculation has run wild since, but guesses center around the rumor that the Catholic Church will be intensely persecuted in the Last Days, and that the End Time Pope will perhaps indeed suffer martyrdom. Today, this secret lies in the Vatican archives.

Whoever this False Prophet is, he will be the Antichrist's staunchest ally. He's the one who convinces everybody to go along with the Mark of the Beast. Then three and a half years after signing the peace pact with Israel, this Dictator, riding on the crest of public admiration, will go to Jerusalem, enter the Temple of Solomon, and seat himself down upon the throne. He will proclaim himself to be God, and will demand worship.

This event, known as the "Abomination of the Desolation," will be the great warning sign that Armageddon is about to begin.

All Hell will break loose, for it is here that four of the Bible's most notorious characters are unleashed upon the Earth: The Four Horsemen of the Apocalypse (Rev. 6). They are perhaps the most widely-known and least understood horrors of the Book of Revelation. The End Time years will see them ride across the landscape, one by one, like a bad dream. The turmoil that will rage, and the environmental disasters that follow, will wipe nearly all human life off the planet. Civilization as we know it will crumble. Only Divine Intervention, it would seem, will prevent Earth's total destruction.

As for this Dictator sitting upon the throne of God, it now becomes clear that he was the first dreaded Horseman. Riding upon the White Horse "with bow and crown," but no arrows, he had an empty quiver, and brought with him a false peace. But the White Horse is Conquest, for those who did bow before this Beast.

"It should have been made public in 1960, but because of its troubling content, and to dissuade the superpowers from undertaking wars, my predecessors in the papal chair have chosen the diplomatic way. All Christians should be content in the knowledge that the oceans will inundate whole continents, and millions of people will die from one moment to the next. Hearing this, people should not long for the rest of the secret. Pray, pray, and do not inquire any more. Everything else should be entrusted to the Holy Mother of God."

Pope John Paul II - 1980

Immediately after this Leader declares himself to be God, the Red Horse will be unleashed upon the Earth. "With sword and power in its girth," this Red Horse, the color of bloodshed, is Slaughter, and now, the very thing that Mankind feared most is upon them—war.

This apocalyptic war will begin with an invasion of the state of Israel by the "king of the south," believed to be the Arab States, most notably Egypt, traditionally the leader of the Arab world. Apparently the Moslem nation will not take to the idea of Israel rebuilding their temple and reinstituting their sacrifices.

The Arab world and Moslem Africa will reinstitute their *jihad* ("Holy War"), and attack the state of Israel. The Bible, however, gives ominous passage to Egypt, warning of a terrible judgement that will befall them in the last days: "The waters of the Nile shall be dried up" (Isaiah 19:5), and after all, Egypt is a gift of the Nile.

Then the "king of the north" will use this chaos to launch his own attack of Israel (some believe in an overwhelming double-cross of Egypt). Most Biblical scholars have named Russia as the dreaded Magog "from the uttermost north." As it stands today, the Russian military is in shambles, but this "Magog" will have a number of allies gathered around it when it does invade the state of Israel.

This will be the unleashing of the Black Horse—Famine— for now the effects of this war are to be felt worldwide. Once the Mid-East oil stops flowing, trucks will stop rolling, and it will quickly become a hand-to-mouth existence for every citizen in every industrialized country. This rider holds "a pair of balances" in his hand, as if weighing what is owed.

The Book of Revelation forewarns Russia that they will in turn be defeated, and that their homeland will become a "lake of fire" (Ezekiel 39:6). Lindsey believes that this powerful Russian alliance will be subdued by the combined efforts of the EU and "the kings of the east."

China. The most populous nation on Earth (1.3 billion people), and the fastest developing economy in the world. China, however, has two big problems facing it:

(1) Family Planning: "Number 1 difficulty under heaven." China is grossly overpopulated, and growing. Strict laws (one child for urban families, two for rural families) have succeeded in lowering the birth rate, but this has still greater consequences than is at first apparent. In a country that places great emphasis on honoring their ancestors, soon an entire generation of children will be growing up without relatives.

(2) China's second problem: There aren't enough women. Current estimates show that seventy million Chinese soldiers alone are without women, certainly an uncomfortable and dangerous male-to-female ratio.

Let's see—a rising giant—no aunts or uncles—no women. "Wars are best fought by young men with raging hormones" goes the old saying. World economists forecast that the 21st century will see this sleeping Dragon awakened, and show its teeth.

Lindsey believes that it will be after the EU and China unite to defeat the Russian forces that a funny thing happens: the waters of the Euphrates River dry up "that the way of the kings of the east might be prepared" (Rev. 9:14).

This may not be as supernatural as one might think. There are dozens of dams along the Euphrates. According to Revelation, when the Euphrates River (1800 miles in length) is dry, China will use the occasion to launch an invasion across the dried riverbed against the Roman Dictator in a challenge for world domination. Revelation 9:16 states that this army will number "two hundred thousand thousand." If true, this incredible multitude of two hundred million men would be the largest army ever to march into battle.

"A terrifying prophecy is made about the destiny of this Asian horde," writes Lindsey. "They will wipe out one-third of the Earth's population (Rev. 9:18). The phenomenon by which this destruction of life will take place are given: it will be by fire, smoke and brimstone (melted earth). The thought may have occurred to you that this is strikingly similar to the phenomena associated with thermonuclear warfare. In fact, many Bible expositors believe that this is an accurate first-century description of a twentieth-century thermonuclear war."

This would be the release of the last horseman, the Pale Horse ("chloros"), the sickish color of disease, from too many dead to bury. For this rider's name is Death. He will kill by sword (weapon), and hunger (famine), and "with the beasts of the Earth." Until now, animals have always held a supernatural fear of Mankind, but in the End Times, the animals of the Earth will no longer fear man, and they will attack at will.

Chinese leaders, however, claim that even nuclear weapons cannot stop human wave tactics. Lindsey writes, "In this day of H-bombs and super weapons, it seems incredible that there could ever be another

0.16 seconds after the first nuclear explosion on Earth (Courtesy of U.S. Department of Energy)

great land war fought by basically conventional means, yet the Chinese believe that with a vastly superior numerical force, they can absorb losses and still win a war. They also believe that all war is still determined on the ground by land forces."

Mao Tse-tung was quoted as saying that using atom bombs on two hundred million land forces would be like throwing pebbles at ants.

And where does the United States fit into this prophecy?

"This isn't an easy question to answer," writes Lindsey in his book *The 1980s: Countdown To Armageddon* (Bantam, 1981), "because there are no specific or even indirect references to America in Bible prophecy. However, there are things we do know from which we can make some deductions:

"First, prophecy singles out who the leader of the western world will be in the final stage of history—and it won't be the

U.S. As we have seen already, the ten-nation confederacy will be the west's dominating power.

"It is possible that the U.S. would remain a world power if we became an equal ally of the European confederation. In that way, with each dependent on the other, America could keep much of its sovereignty and freedom. But it is clear that the U.S. cannot be the leader in the future. The past has shown that the U.S. is not a reliable ally."

Ultimately, we will have only two great powers left to fight the climatic battle of Armageddon: the powerful Roman Dictator versus the vast hordes of the Chinese war machine.

The Book of Revelation tells us that this Final Showdown between East and West will be in the Middle East, in a valley known as Har Megiddo ("to slay"), but warns that all the cities of the world will be destroyed. Mountains will be blown off the map, entire islands will sink, and one-third of our waters will be poisoned by a star named Wormwood which falls into the sea (Rev. 8:11). Wormwood is the English translation for the Russian word Chernobyl, perhaps implying that the seas will be radioactive.

Everything built by man will crumble before his eyes, and as this horrendous battle of Armageddon rises to its awful climax, and just when it appears that Mankind is about to annihilate himself—the "Son of man" returns to put the end to the war of all wars. "Behold he comes with clouds; and every eye shall see him" (Rev. 1:7; Dan. 7:13).

The Christ Messiah will arrive at the Mount of Olives, and the instant that his foot touches ground, the mountain will split in two, resulting in a great earthquake. This will bring an abrupt halt to the wave of destruction taking place across the Earth. It will be the Apocalypse—"to unveil what was hidden."

"And they shall beat their swords into plowshares, and their spears into pruning hooks; nation shall not lift up sword against nation, neither shall they learn war any more" (Isaiah 2:4).

I was able to interview Lindsey after watching a live taping of his weekly TV show *The International Intelligence Briefing* at TBN Studios in Costa Mesa, California. He's a distinguished-looking man who's been in the public eye for almost three

Hal Lindsey and author

decades. I told him that I had been in contact with his publishing company for five months trying to capture this interview.

"I receive thousands of letters a month requesting interviews," Lindsey replied. "I don't have time to read the requests, let alone answer them."

Indeed, in the dozen or so books on Armageddon that I read in my research, I doubt that there were more than two that did not refer to Lindsey and his book. With this in mind, I asked him whether he had changed his mind about his interpretation of any of the prophecies he wrote about so long ago.

"Not at all. The very things I wrote about back then are coming to pass right before our eyes this very day. I believe we're headed for a great crisis."

About America, you write: "Let us get about the business of prayer to preserve the nation." Considering our apparent lack of prayer, what advice would you have for our country concerning this coming new millennium?

"I think in the coming millennium, it'll be more a question of survival. The destruction from a thermonuclear war will be so complete that the only thing we'll be able to do is pray."

Speak a little on China, that great dragon of one billion people, looming like a giant on the global economic market.

> "China is now more dangerous than it's ever been, not only in its growing arsenal, but in the selling of its technology to lesser nations. They have put the whole world in peril. The mere fact that two countries, such as India and Pakistan, would use actual nuclear blasts to threaten one another shows us that the idea of MAD [Mutually Assured Destruction] is not going to be enough to prevent a nuclear war."

Have you met Pope John Paul II? And more importantly, what do you know about that Third Secret of Fatima?

> "I've never met the Pope, but from what I understand from Malachi Martin [a former Jesuit priest, author, and expert on Vatican affairs] is that not the next pope after Pope John Paul II, but the pope after him will be the Antichrist. So naturally, the Catholic Church does not want to release that information."

[This coincides with St. Malachy, the eleventh-century Irish monk, who prophesied all future popes by their coats-of-arms from 1143 A.D. to "the end of the world." Only two more coats-of-arms are listed after Pope John Paul II: *Gloria Olivae* ("The Glory of the Olive"), and *Petrus Romanus* "after which the seven-hilled city will be destroyed and the dreadful Judge will judge the people."]

Mr. Lindsey, in your book *The 1980s: Countdown To Armageddon*, you write: "It's my opinion that UFOs are real and that there will be a proven 'close encounter of the third kind' soon. And I believe the source of this phenomenon is some type of alien being of great intelligence and power.

> "According to the Bible, a demon is a spiritual personality in a state of war with God. I believe these demons will stage a spacecraft

landing on Earth. They will claim to be from an advanced culture in another galaxy. They may even claim to the have 'seeded' human life on this planet. If these demons led by Satan, their chief, did pull off such a deception, then they could certainly lead the world into total error regarding God and His revelation."

Are you suggesting that these non-human beings could be Lucifer and his Fallen Angels, cast out from Heaven so long ago?

"I do believe that UFOs are demonic. Prophecy tells us that demons will be allowed to use their powers of deception in a grand way during the last days of history. And if Mankind can create a hologram, think of what a demon could do to deceive the human race."

And yet—Rev. 21:2 reads: "And I, John, saw the holy city, new Jerusalem, coming down from God out of heaven." Four times he mentions this great "city of God" that descends down from the skies. This celestial city is going to hover over Earth for one thousand years while the Messiah continues ruling from Jerusalem. This is a very cosmic image of the city of God. Sounds suspiciously like a UFO to me.

"No, I believe that's a wrong interpretation. This 'city of God' will not be a UFO, and it will not be a hologram. It will be a definite city."

Driving home on the crowded L.A. freeway system, I had a thought about Armageddon: If the planet does end up in a thermonuclear war, and we are not saved by Divine Intervention, the survivors will be doomed to a Nuclear Winter. The freezing cold of a long dark winter would leave the Earth barren of civilization and nearly denuded of life. A frozen planet would be a world in which very little would survive.

And even if this nuclear Armageddon does not take place,

the consensus among the scientific community is that the full force of global warming from the Greenhouse Effect is due to hit this planet in about forty years. The melting Antarctic glaciers will raise the sea levels an apocalyptic twenty-six feet. Coastlines will change. Islands will disappear. And perhaps most disturbing of all is the report that even if there were a concerted effort to ward off the Greenhouse Effect, we would only succeed in postponing the inevitable for perhaps another forty years.

So in a sinister irony, Mr. Lindsey, we need this dreaded Antichrist to saddle up and ride. His very appearance over the horizon will signify the threshold of a new and more enlightened age.

We must also consider that we are a carbon-based Universe. The carbon atom contains six neutrons, six electrons, six protons. 666. So maybe we are our own Antichrists.

Either way, it's the Antichrist versus the Messiah. We all know that the Messiah wins. So here's my question: If two-thirds of the Earth's population is to be killed off, one-half of all mountains blown off the map, and one-third of the waters poisoned—why does the Messiah wait so long to get here?

Long after I finished writing this review, something still gnawed away inside of me. I couldn't stop thinking about how somewhere in the world, a future Dictator is walking the streets. Biding his time, perhaps, but waiting for fate to call his name. It's prophesied that our children will come to think of him as the "Beast." We'll allow him to take the world by storm.

I'd like to think that we're too smart for that, but I've got a funny feeling we aren't.

The Late Great Planet Earth
(Zondervan Publishing House, 1970)
Hal Lindsey

For a listing of books and tapes, write to:
Western Front Publishing
2275 San Ysidro Drive
Beverly Hills, California 90210

For information on Lindsey's
International Intelligence Briefing,
check your local television listings, or
www.iib-report.com

Epilogue

The UFO phenomenon may be a lot like Rock Soup. This is where the poor man comes to town, and no one will feed him, and so he says, "That's okay. I'll make some Rock Soup." He starts up a fire and boils some water in a pot, then puts in many small pebbles and one nice-sized rock.

Some of the villagers gather around to watch, and so the poor man admits, well, the whole affair would taste better with a clove of garlic. So someone hands him one, he carefully chops it up and tosses it into the boiling water.

To make a long story short, any good soup, even Rock Soup, demands the Three Blessings: carrots, celery and onions. So a couple of spectators bless the soup, the poor man chops them up, and tosses them into the pot.

Cutting to the chase, the poor man now has a perfect stock as he stirs his boiling rocks, so someone tosses in a potato so as not to waste a good broth. By now, the soup is done and everyone's mouth is watering, and so the poor man ladles out a bowl of Rock Soup for every one of them, making sure that each bowl contains a small pebble, then he ladles himself a nice big bowl of Rock Soup, and together they sup.

The UFO phenomenon can be likened to Rock Soup in that everyone has been throwing their blessings. The resulting soup is what we bring to it. Even the doubters who throw in their skepticism help to make it the bubbling froth that it is.

But where's the beef?

America has turned out to be a wonderful silly place to live. Freedom can do that to the sense of humor, where anything goes. And where else in the world are you free to rise up from the bottom and own land like you can in America?

At the time of the American Revolution, there were only two universities in all of England, but there were already nine colleges in the American colonies. The USA will one day go down as the Greatest Nation in the history of Great Nations, and it will be her opportunity of an education for all that will prove to be her greatest contribution to the world. More and more, we come to see that knowledge is power.

This has been the American Century, and the Age of Speed. Within the short span of one hundred years, the USA has taken us from the horse-and-buggy to a man on the moon. And it's the American dollar bill that has those three Latin words inscribed upon it: *Novus Ordo Seclorum* - "A New Order of the Age." With the image of the Single Eye floating above the Great Pyramid, seeing America into this New Age...

This book presents us with two seemingly unanswered questions: (1) Are we being visited by aliens? (2) If so, are they friendly? Perhaps to best understand the future, we must first take a look at the past. Here then is a brief history of Mankind:

Somewhere in the Stone Age, what scholars consider to

be the first true man emerged - *Homo erectus* - "he who stood upright." He wasn't too bright and he was afraid of fire. Where he came from, no one knows, but he died out about one million years ago.

Then about 100,000 years ago, Neanderthal Man suddenly appeared - *Homo sapiens* - "he who is filled with knowledge." He lived in caves, but cooked with fire and buried his dead. Still, scholars insist that he was "more ape than man, more man than ape," and not in direct line of human descent. Neanderthal Man also went extinct, never to be seen again.

Then about 30,000 years ago, around the end of our last Ice Age, Cro-Magnon Man appeared, out of the blue, and with a brain full of knowledge that far surpassed Neanderthal Man. He is considered "Modern Man," our direct ancestor. This Cro-Magnon Man settled down and planted crops, built cities and wrote books. Of course, for theologian and archeologist alike, the puzzle is: Where did this Cro-Magnon Man spring from? Like Neanderthal Man before us, we seemed to have appeared from nowhere.

That's about all that we know for sure. There's a Missing Link in there somewhere. And now that the planet has grown smaller, and the human race appears to be heading towards critical mass, many believe that we are about to come face to face with this Missing Link. A "Messiah" will descend from the skies in time to ward off our demons. Our planet will somehow achieve yoga ("union") with the Universe.

We must also keep in mind that Mankind is a proud species. There is an ancient fable about the greedy man to whom Zeus decided to grant any wish he wanted, on the condition that his neighbor would receive twice as much. This man, unable to bear the thought of another person having better luck than he, wished to lose an eye!

So there may be no dealing with Earthling's hubris.

We shall see.

Boldface indicates illustrations

BOOK ORDER FORM

AOA
P R E S S

california

To order directly from the publisher,
send $19.95 + $4.00 S&H to:

AOA Press
P.O. Box 572377
Tarzana, CA 91357

Send check or money order payable to AOA Press.
Be sure to include your name and mailing address.
California residents please include 8.25% sales tax.

To Order Toll Free
1-800-700-4024
VISA • MasterCard • Discover

Please photocopy this form

Please send me _____ copy(ies) of *Aliens Over America*

Name_____

Address_____

City_____State_____ Zip_____

Trade-sized paperback
259 pages • over 70 illustrations
ISBN: 0-9675632-0-8

Thank you for your order